Why We Left the Left

Personal Stories by Leftists/Liberals Who Evolved to Embrace Libertarianism

Compiled and edited by

Tom Garrison

An ebook version of *Why We Left the Left* was originally published in July 2012. This is a print edition of that ebook.

Address all inquiries to Tom Garrison at:
whywelefttheleft@yahoo.com

Visit the Why We Left the Left Facebook page.
Your comments are welcome.

Published by CreateSpace Independent Publishing Platform
First Edition

St. George, Utah

Copyright 2013

ISBN 978-1492279570

Why We Left the Left
Contents

Dedication

I want to acknowledge three people without whose influence my life would not take the course it did. First, two professors at California State University (then college) at Bakersfield, California—the late Dr. Charles McCall and the late Dr. William Hanson. Charles was the "hard" quantitative data-loving, Burkian conservative political scientist and Bill the liberal, "soft" data sociologist. During my undergraduate years both pushed me, in different yet equally important ways, to understand, analyze, and challenge one's assumptions. Good teachers and good friends.

Finally, my deepest gratitude and love to Deborah Looker, my wife since 1982. She read and commented on every essay in this collection—her editing and general comments were crucial to my work. Even more valuable was her tolerance for the hours I spent in front of a computer screen and my yapping about the book contributors and related matters.

Introduction

One political question intrigues almost everyone who studies, participates, or is interested in politics: "Why do people identify with a certain ideology and/or political party?" Numerous scholarly and popular books examine political ideology/party identification and why certain ideologies attract certain individuals. This book examines that question in two separate, yet joined phases. Why do people initially identify with the Left/liberalism and why do these same individuals abandon that ideology to evolve into libertarians? This inquiry is unique in its focus on former liberals/leftists who become libertarians.

Included are 23 stories from Americans and one Irishman, baring at least part of their souls to answer these questions. All contributors at one point identified with the Left/liberalism. Each explains what originally drew them to the left part of the political spectrum. Virtually all mention some version of the popular stereotype of liberals/leftists "caring for the average person." And all came to see that as a wispy apparition, based more on intention than fact.

A common theme for why the liberals/leftists abandoned their ideology is the ugly discovery of the inherent elitism of leftists/liberals. Over and over in these stories, the contributors give examples of their liberal/leftist "comrades" explaining how they (liberals/leftists) are needed to steer the people in the proper direction, for their own good of course. The true believing leftists/liberals cling to this illusion. Through many different paths, the contributors to this volume come to see the anti-democratic, elitist nature of this belief.

An equally common denominator is the lack of respect for, or even acknowledgement of, personal responsibility in ones behavior. A core value of the Left/liberalism is victimhood. Everyone—women, gays and lesbians, people of color, public employee union members, the working class, and so on—is an actual or potential victim. As such, any dysfunctional behavior can always be excused as the result of societal oppression, racism and sexism, rich people and capitalists, corporations, "the man", and on and on. Of course, negative external forces do exist, but they are not *always* (or even most of the time) the cause of crappy behavior or failure. Many of the stories in this book note that this refusal to acknowledge personal responsibility strongly influenced the contributor to turn away from the Left/liberalism.

Disillusionment with the notion that government action is needed for every problem—real or imagined—is inherent in turning from leftism/liberalism to libertarianism. Several contributors expound upon this theme.

Many contributors also cite the power of classical liberal economic theory—truly free markets—as a factor in their leaving the Left. Real world examples of the failure of socialist/welfare state economic policy became too difficult to ignore.

Finally, a minor, yet telling, theme is the lack of humor or playfulness in liberals and the Left. Several contributors note the feeling of liberation once they rejected the dour self-importance of the Left/liberalism.

One popular conception of libertarians is that they are, for the most part, disgruntled old white guys. While that group is represented, more than 25 percent of the stories are from women and more than two-thirds are by people younger than 50. This gender and generational diversity extends to occupations—contributors include college students, law students, an attorney, a professional artist, public school teachers, a chemist, writers, a filmmaker, a law professor, a stay-at-home mom, a firefighter, the CEO of a $40 million company, a TV reporter, an editor, the CEO of a free market environmental think tank, and a research engineer.

The contributors understanding of libertarianism is equally diverse. Some have steeped themselves in classical liberal/libertarian literature, while others got their first taste by listening to libertarian talk shows. Some are Libertarian Party members, some are not. All identify as libertarians.

While 23 diverse stories, no matter how compelling, cannot fully answer the questions posed above, these personal narratives do provide insight. As noted earlier, there are common themes. These typical

Americans and one Irishman became libertarians via different paths, but all, to use a simplistic yet true phrase, support free markets and free minds.

It behooves liberals and leftists to read this book if they are at all interested in serious critiques of their ideology. The contributors are not life-long conservatives taking one more shot at their leftist/liberal enemies. These folks are former "fellow travelers". If liberals/leftists have a free mind—which, of course, they all claim—they might learn some useful lessons from the stories of why good people deserted their statist cause.

Conservatives will benefit from these stories because they missed the opportunity to enlist these folks in their movement. The contributors were obviously dissatisfied with the Left/liberalism so why not become conservatives? Perhaps because conservatives, like liberals/leftists, are statists—they simply use state power to control people's behavior in different spheres.

Libertarians can also benefit from reading this book. The contributor's stories will make them aware that the libertarian movement is larger and more diverse than they suspect. That it includes both intellectuals who embraced libertarianism mainly through thought and analysis and those who arrived mostly due to specific personal experiences. Both are necessary and important to any political movement.

If libertarianism is to become something more than a thorn in the side of the major parties it must become relevant for the vast majority of Americans. The contributors to this book reflect average people. No celebrities here. These are people who realize, in the words of Matt Welch and Nick Gillespie, that "People acting peacefully, mostly left to their own devices and not empowered by the state to force others into servitude, will create riches far more meaningful and vast than the cramped business of tax-collecting, regulation-spewing, do-as-I-say-or-else governments." (*Reason*, August/September 2011. p. 38)

Anyone paying attention to politics knows there is a battle for America's future. The choices are stark—more and more liberal/leftist supported government intervention; the nanny state dictating economic and personal behavior; the destruction of initiative and self-respect; welfare for mooching individuals and corporations; and so on. The contributors have seen both sides—they chose liberty.

It is my fervent hope that this collection of stories will hasten the day when libertarianism is widely recognized for what it is—the political movement for adults.

Matthew T. Austin
Attorney and solo-practitioner; East Rochester, NY

Matthew T. Austin, Esq. is an attorney and solo-practitioner in East Rochester, New York. He is a political junky and has a tendency to throw things at his television. Matthew enjoys debating philosophy, politics, and art. He is learning to play golf and can't understand why people think the sport is relaxing. Matthew currently lives with his fiancée, Nichole. Their two cats, Sophie Fatale and Socrates, are a source of much frustration and love.

A Portrait of the Leftist as a Young Man
by
Matthew T. Austin, Esq.

Why did I leave the Left? I turned my back on leftism because I experienced the consequences of a collectivist ideology. I believe that collectivism does violence to the very essence of the individual. It was my experiences with collectivism, my philosophical explorations, and my own struggle to make ends meet that made me realize that there is a fundamental disconnection between what I am qua human—a being of intrinsic value—and the Left's utopian hope. I have seen some of the sweetest and kindest of the flower-children, snarl, spit, and hiss like Gollum grasping for Sauron's Ring when the flaws in their argument were exposed. This occurs because the collectivist's identity is wrapped in their cause—they perceive any challenge to their ideology as a personal attack.

To answer the question, "why I left the Left" requires a brief explanation as to why I became a communist. You see, growing up, I was a typical angst-ridden youth, but also a student eager to learn. I was a bright, albeit misguided, kid; very rebellious and I looked upon "The System" with disdain and outright contempt. In other words, I was a walking cliché. But how I got there is important. I recognized something early on as a junior high student. I saw that the world was an unfair place, as teachers, parents, and other students treated each other unjustly. Indeed, I was often the target of some of this inequity. As a budding intellectual with a strong sense of the intrinsic value of a human being, I sought to understand why such inequity exists. In my search for truth, I discovered three copies of the *Communist Manifesto* in my school library. Channeling Abbie Hoffman (without knowing anything about him just yet), I stole a copy and read it.

Why these books were located in my school library without F.A. Hayek's *Road to Serfdom* to counter balance the inquiry is a discussion for another day.

I read the *Communist Manifesto* on my own at 15. Without the guidance of a philosophically trained mind to challenge the ideas contained in the book, I absorbed the ideas as fact. The public school I attended did not help me in this matter either. In fact, my senior year economics class did not discuss the foundations of capitalism at all. As I recall we watched a cartoon about the stock market and watched parts of Michael Moore's "Roger and Me". As you can probably guess, my "education" confirmed what I had been reading.

As a result of this lack of critical inquiry I became a Marxist: everything made sense through the prism of class warfare. The school administrators, the teachers, and the rich kids were all part of the ruling capitalist elite and I, as the son of blue-collar worker, was a member of the proletariat. All of the problems I was facing as a teenager were not my fault: I was being exploited by the capitalist system. (Clearly, my teenage angst had nothing to do with my social anxiety disorder, my profusely pocked-marked pimple face, or that I routinely played Dungeons & Dragons; it was the fault of the bourgeoisie). The revelation that I need not take responsibility for my own inadequacies energized me and I devoured as much literature on the subject as I could.

It also helped that, when I publicly announced myself as a communist, it aggravated the establishment. Also, girls with the same sense of rebellion (i.e. angst) as I started paying attention to me.

I read many of Vladimir Lenin's works, such as *The April Theses* and *The State and the Revolution*. I loved to debate these ideas with my friends, and I think I had some of them convinced. We engaged in late night debates on the subject of the concentration of capital, the exploitation of labor, and the possibilities of a utopian communist society. These conversations, of course, happened every Friday night at the local Denny's while we drank our capitalist coffee, smoked our capitalist cigarettes, and made sure we were home by midnight because our bourgeois moms wanted the capitalist car home by then.

Fast-forward a few years and I'm a member of the proletariat, freedom fighter and revolutionary without much of a career to speak of, a broken down car and no money—not that money was important to me of course, I was, after all, trapped in the system. But I decided to go back to school to get a better understanding of how the corporate elite were holding people like me down, why I couldn't get a better salary flipping burgers at Denny's, and why I couldn't smoke all the pot that I wanted.

Prior to going back to school, I took a few philosophy classes during the time I wasted at Finger Lakes Community College and I liked the philosophical approach to life. (I still do, in fact). The pursuit of truth was my real motivation for returning to school. And that is the single most important thing to understand from my story to answer the question as to why I left the Left. When I went back to school, I wanted to study philosophy; I wanted to seek the truth.

I believed then, as I do now, that Truth, (with a capital "T") exists. Contradictions cannot exist, as Ayn Rand so famously reiterated. (I say reiterated for it was Aristotle who expressed the one rule at the very heart of logic, the Law of the Excluded Middle). Nothing is relative. There is but one truth and the human race will discover it at some point. If you see areas of gray when viewing a socio-political problem (or any problem for that matter), then you are not being discerning enough. The discovery of truth requires a continual dialectic between propositions, positions, policies, and philosophical ideas. Without that dialectic, without that back and forth discussion, truth cannot be found. But more importantly, understanding cannot be attained. To understand the very heart of an issue is the first step on the road to discovery and real progress. My commitment to the dialectic would end up being the hammer that smashed the collectivist looking glass I had been using for years.

My first months back in college were great. I had been accepted by the prestigious State University of New York (SUNY) at Geneseo. I was an "older student" and I was instantly popular because I could buy beer for all the eighteen-year olds. While they drank cheap beer, I filled their heads with how the bourgeois elites exploited the proletariat, like me (even though the "system" provided me loans to attend college). My classes were tough, but I was being exposed to more ideas and new concepts. To be clear, while I attended SUNY Geneseo there were no shortage of leftwing professors. Indeed, there

14

was a dearth of libertarian or conservative professors in the History and English departments. As I recall, a particular professor (who I would grow to have a deep enmity for) began her class each semester by pronouncing that she was a "Marxist-feminist" and if you didn't agree with her, you would surely fail. Most professors, to be fair, were less overt in their bias. They just fancied themselves akin to Robin Williams' portrayal of a beatnik professor in "The Dead Poets Society." (I don't recall, however, if any of them stood on tables while preaching the death of truth). The philosophy department was different; the professors truly embraced the notion of an open mind. But I will discuss the department later, as the philosophy department was critical in my paradigm shift.

Within a semester I got involved in liberal politics on campus. I attended meetings and teach-ins sponsored by the Democratic Socialists. At this time I finally learned about Abbie Hoffman and I could confidently say that I was already in tune with Abbie's message. Indeed, I had expanded on his thesis by stealing more than just books: food from a local grocery store chain (a very bourgeois food outlet), utensils from Denny's, and beer from rival frat houses. I also became involved in the anti-war movement and participated in many a "rally" where we marched up and down the school's quad (all 500 feet of it) screaming over everyone else: "This is what democracy looks like!"

Clearly, the irony was lost on us.

I also got involved in a poetry-performance art troupe called InnerRhythms. InnerRhythms had prided itself for being an avant-garde group that consisted of musicians, poets, writers, artists and, unfortunately, activists. I say "unfortunately" because as time went on, the original purpose of the group, exalting Art qua Art, was supplanted by a hard left critique of the War in Iraq, society, and everyone opposed to the Cultural Left's weltanschauung.

I loved InnerRhythms. I loved being a part of an organization that provided a means of expression for me. I loved being immersed in a community that helped define the counter-culture on Geneseo's campus. Every week the group's members would gather to discuss philosophy, art, poetry, and music. We shared with each other original works of art, critiqued our work, and just laughed and shared our love of expression. We hosted weekly open-mics to present our work and encouraged others to express themselves. At the end of every semester the organization put together a performance art showcase for the campus.

Initially, nothing was too taboo to tackle as a topic of discussion and inspiration could come from anywhere. The art we presented ranged from the spiritual to the darkly psychological. Unfortunately, our popularity and the unique platform we provided for the community would transform InnerRhythms into a propaganda apparatus for the anti-war Left. Instead of artistic themes, the group started moving toward cultural critiques, and of course, the evil of George W. Bush. Needless to say, college Republicans and conservative types never attended our open-mics, even though they would most certainly be welcome! (We were open-minded you see). However, as the group's message became increasingly political, any ideas that were contrary to the core message became taboo.

This is the most embarrassing part of my days in Geneseo: how mind-numbingly close-minded we had become. It really was an echo chamber. The marches, the teach-ins, and the protesting went on without any critical discussion. Our group discussions were really just a bunch of lefties sitting around and complaining about how unfair and awful America had become, notwithstanding their cushy upper middle-class backgrounds. This ignorance reached its zenith when the leftists groups held an anti-war week where a few teachers vented their frustrations by extolling conspiracy theories regarding the Bush Administration's reasons for invading Iraq. Dissent is patriotic—a sentiment I certainly agree with—but, looking back at the level of uncritical reaction to the war in Iraq and the Bush Administration's policies leaves me to wonder: just where is the line between patriotic dissent and outright sedition?

My experience at Geneseo was not all leftwing politics. As I mentioned earlier, the philosophical life was one that I had grown to love and I became active with the philosophy department. I revitalized the Philosophy Club and we routinely held student run discussion groups on topics that ranged from "What is Feminism?" to "Identity and Free Will". I made it a point to approach other academic groups and have them join in the discussion. I believed that everyone's voice mattered. (I still do, in fact).

Needless to say the juxtaposition of my work as a philosophy student and my political activities had created a tension within me that couldn't be ignored.

The cracks in my paradigm as a communist began when I started witnessing the actions of my comrades not quite lining up with what they were preaching. For example, the Democratic Socialists changed their name to the Student Progressive Action Committee (SPAC) in order to attract new members. The leaders believed that the word "socialist" would scare independents away. I was exasperated with the leadership. Why would we want to hide the fact that we were socialists? Isn't socialism the better socio-political model? This was not a line of argumentation they cared to consider; what mattered was growing their numbers for protests and direct action. To this day, I still don't know what they meant by "direct action."

Then there was the time I saw a custodian cursing softly to himself as he attempted to scrub graffiti off of a stone wall in the middle of January. Geneseo, located in upstate New York, would get very cold during the month of January. I remember stopping briefly as the biting wind whipped past me and watched the custodian shiver in the cold in order to scrub away the anti-Republican vitriol painted upon the stone wall. I remember feeling an intense feeling of guilt. I wasn't the one who sprayed the graffiti, but I felt responsible nonetheless. Isn't this guy the type of person we are supposed to be fighting for?

This property damage was not necessarily isolated. To be true, it was not widespread; the leftists weren't as hardcore as they claimed to be. Most of the graffiti was limited to juvenile limericks about George W. Bush on bathroom stall walls. The worst example, however, was when some unknown activist spread a chemical on the quad to kill the grass to form a basic message: "Think." That sad and awful truth was that the activist misspelled "think" and caused the campus, already

17

cash strapped, to expend significant amounts of money to repair the damage. It was an embarrassment for everyone.

The cracks in my paradigm erupted into outright fissures when I was invited by a number of philosophy professors to join in their monthly book club. I was ecstatic! I would get to debate philosophy with the professors in a private setting! The first book I read for the club was Edmund Burke's *Reflections on the Revolution in France*. The ideas contained in that book challenged me in ways my history and English professors never did. Because I wanted to make a good first impression, I devoured the book to the exclusion of all others. I took notes and I prepared to discuss and debate on whatever topic the professors felt relevant.

I wasn't prepared, however, for what happened at my first meeting with them.

We met at a local, upscale bar called the Big Tree Inn. The group included a professor from the School of Business, a philosophy professor, and two adjunct philosophy professors who were still working on their doctorates. They welcomed me, bought me a drink and began discussing the possibilities of liberation for the Middle East as a result of the American invasion of Afghanistan and Iraq.

What!? I thought we were there for oil?

The rest of the evening was a flurry of libertarian and conservative arguments for and against the war. These arguments were influenced by the reading for the night. Would a radical revolutionary act, like the American invasion, create the seeds of a real democracy, or would it devolve into a France-styled terror as Edmund Burke criticized? I sat there quietly absorbing the arguments, my mouth hanging open in Neanderthal fashion, as all of this was new to me. When my opinion was asked, I suggested (I didn't shout) that perhaps oil was the real reason for being in Iraq. I knew that this was not going to be accepted as a good response, so I braced for the rebuke. (I actually contorted my face into a wince). What happened was unexpected: the professors nodded at my response and then began probing me for more information. They asked hard questions concerning human nature, the role of America in the world, the conflict of ideas in the context of history, and the very nature of injustice. Many of these questions I couldn't answer with my memorized slogans and chants. But each question was designed to better understand my position, not to castigate me for being different. The professors at this club treated me with a respect that I certainly wouldn't have given any Republican or Libertarian (read: capitalist pig).

At the end of the night, they invited me to their next meeting. For the rest of the semester, I met with them about four other times and I was exposed to libertarian and conservative politics. I started learning, on my own, about F.A. Hayek and Milton Freidman. I read Michael Oakshott and Dinesh D'sousa. I started reading *Reason* magazine regularly. I was so enthralled by what I was reading that I applied for a scholarship through the Institute for Humane Studies and attended a week long summer seminar in California. The seminar's focus: Liberty and Society.

We spent the week discussing the imperfect nature of mankind, the corrupting influence of power, and the benefits of a decentralized government. This is what I should've learned all those years ago when I saw the inequities occurring around me. It is the concentration of political power and the stifling of individual expression that causes injustice, not a vaguely described "capitalist elite." Unleashing the creative potential of mankind requires the free individual to be free from constraint.

The seminar was attended by scholars from all across the globe. During that week I met several students from former Soviet States that talked about what it was like during the last days of communism. I spoke with an environmentalist from Tajikistan, discussed art with punk rockers from Sweden, and the free-market with an Objectivist from Belarus. Everyone contributed to the discussion. By the end of that week, I was a changed man.

When I returned from this seminar with a bunch of new ideas in tow, I couldn't wait to discuss with my comrades where true freedom lies. Embracing the free market is an embrace of the individual and creativity; the contrary is to control the individual and stifle progress. If liberation was what we wanted, we needed to reject socialism, communism and all its permutations. I soon learned, however, that liberation isn't exactly what the Left was looking for.

My fall from grace before the leftwing community began at a party following an InnerRhythms performance. As per the usual, all of the prominent leftists and hangers-on were in attendance. The leaders of the newly renamed Student Progressive Action Committee had graciously hosted the party. And, as per the usual, I was engaging in philosophical debate around the keg. This time, however, I was armed with a libertarian arsenal. One of the leaders of SPAC grew annoyed with me, claimed I was being way too loud and suggested we move the discussion outside. Once outside he and I were joined by the other members of the SPAC's leadership.

With the backdrop of a college party going on, I was questioned by the leadership. But their questions felt more like an interrogation. Their questions were not the same type of probing questions designed to flesh out an interlocutor's position. The three of them seemed deeply concerned with my own questioning and were probing for something else. I felt like I was being accused of something. I felt like I was being accused for doing what I have been trained to do as a philosopher: seek the truth and challenge all propositions.

The conversation eventually turned to the role of the individual in society. I made a number of arguments regarding the pursuit of happiness and the need for liberty to achieve our maximum potential. With a smirk, I was told: "Freedom is not a property of the individual; it is a property of the State."

My reaction was quite visceral and immediate. I shouted "that's tyranny!" After my reaction, without skipping a beat, I was told that my view was nothing but "bourgeois hyper-individualism."

At that moment, I realized that I just may have been a libertarian my whole life. That, through all of my travels as a musician, philosopher, poet, cook, and political activist, I have always desired the kind of liberty to allow me to be who I wanted, on my own terms. My sense of rebellion was really a simple desire to be.

I remember glancing through the window during the tense silence that settled between the four of us. Through the window I saw the leftist in their army surplus jackets, Che Guevera t-shirts, hippie skirts, and hipster headgear. For the first time I saw what it was that I had become and what I was a part of: one of Lenin's useful idiots. There was no individualism there at all. Everyone at the party was a talking point, a bumper sticker, a crudely painted sign, or a protest chant. Every act of artistic expression, every spoken word was subsumed by the cause, the next protest, the next march. I glanced at the leadership of SPAC and I saw the vanguard: the very people who professed to lead the masses to freedom would squash dissent the moment it became too inconvenient. I finished my beer and left the party mumbling something about "agreeing to disagree".

Over my last year at Geneseo, I distanced myself from the Left. The ideas contained in my work with InnerRhythms weren't being received well. The tone of the organizations I had worked with had grown repressive. In fact, one such group, "InfoShare," told me that my ideas weren't welcome. What little contact I had with my former comrades, generally, revolved around why I changed my mind. These conversations had the feel of an intervention and I decided I had had enough. A few friends became outright hostile. I don't speak with them anymore, nor do I care to.

To be clear, I am "friends" with some of them on Facebook. I don't think they know, precisely, what was going through my mind at that time. I like to think that time heals all wounds and wisdom comes with age. But we really don't speak regularly, if at all. And, to be fair, my isolation originated from not only the Left on campus, but the Right wouldn't have anything to do with me either. And rightly so! I was a big jerk to the college Republicans because I allowed my politics to become my identity. I had been nothing but a bullhorn for the most destructive philosophy of the twentieth century. But more importantly, I had betrayed the very philosophical life I had come to the love.

I left the Left because the Left places politics above the individual's need for understanding. The Left requires obedience and does not provide the intellectual space a person needs to achieve an understanding of their reality. The limited perspective we have on reality requires an open and honest examination of all propositions, even those propositions we may hold sacred. Without this process, the individual cannot achieve their maximum potential. To allow the individual to be subsumed into a collectivist mob only creates banality and stagnation. The Left does not see this. The search for truth, the dialectic and the very reason for an individual's existence is to come to grips with a reality we cannot control and to find an understanding—indeed, a place—within that reality to breathe, create and love.

Steve Baier
Professional Artist; Indianola, IA

Steve Baier is a professional artist who specializes in airbrush. His contemporary pin-up girls have gained popularity with top models and private collectors alike, and his loud floral paintings are also emerging. Steve lends his talents to military charities and those who assist developmentally disabled people. Steve is a lifelong Iowa resident and Iowa Hawkeye fan. When not painting, he also enjoys classic muscle cars, baseball games, rock concerts, BBQ festivals, do-it-yourself projects, and much more. Steve can be reached via his website: www.scbartworks.com or via email: steve@scbartworks.com.

Realism in the Post-Liberal Era
by
Steve Baier

A professional artist who quotes Ronald Reagan, cites Ayn Rand as his favorite author, and is opposed to the National Endowment for the Arts? That's me.

My journey from self-described liberal Democrat to right-leaning Libertarian is best described as one of self-discovery. My core beliefs really did not change drastically. My understanding of politics and philosophy, however, was greatly expanded in a relatively short period of time—and my quest for knowledge continues to this day.

I turned 18 and registered to vote in December 1996. In a move that baffled many members of my family, I chose Independent. That has never changed. But make no mistake, I was a Democrat in every other sense. I come from a family of Democrats—I guess you'd call them Blue Dogs. That's typical in Iowa and the Midwest in general. Most Democrat voters here aren't what you'd call radicals. Lots of conservative values, but staunch Democrats nonetheless. I chose Independent status because I didn't like the idea of being fenced in or being part of a herd. So my non-conformist streak already existed, but at the time I had no political philosophy or belief system. I thought President Clinton was an OK guy; couldn't have told you one thing about his platform.

I still was not politically conscious when I began the Commercial Art Program at Des Moines Area Community College in 1998, but meeting other artsy people meant I was associating mostly with liberals. Politics was not a hot topic of conversation in my circles, but all the usual liberal gospels were generally accepted as absolute truth: Republicans were evil, freedom-hating people who were out to get everyone save for very wealthy whites; Democrats were the champions of the "little guy"; it takes a village; the rich didn't deserve to be so; government was responsible for solving all of your problems; patriotism and love of country was *so* last year; and so on. And so this blissful ignorance continued for a few more years. It should be noted however, that in the 2000 Presidential election, I voted for George W. Bush because I thought Al Gore was a schmuck.

As the 2004 Presidential race started to gear up, I began to get interested in politics for the first time. I started reading op-eds and watching Sunday talk shows. However, I had a severe case of confirmation bias; I generally agreed with anything that praised Democrats. At this time, my career was going nowhere and I was generally unhappy about it. I needed someone to blame for my problems and underachievement (not myself, of course!) and taking an interest in liberal politics made me feel like I was part of something, and together we had a common enemy to rally against. Plus, artists are supposed to be liberals, right? I even attended a John Kerry rally at the Iowa State Fairgrounds. But I began to grow uneasy with Kerry, and *very* uneasy with Edwards. One night I was on a website which had information about all the American political parties, not just the big two. I clicked on something called the Libertarian Party.

These libertarians were talking about small, limited government; individual freedom; sound money policy; non-interventionist foreign policy; and asking for people's opinion of something called Fair Tax. Even when they disagreed with one another, they did so in a respectful manner. My curiosity was piqued and my search continued. I discovered *Reason* magazine, with their slogan, "Free Minds and Free Markets"—and I subscribed. Many libertarians quoted Ronald Reagan and some guy named Goldwater who I had never heard of. Trips to the library ensued. I realized that I was very much in agreement with most libertarian positions, and most libertarians were very much in agreement with the founders of this great nation. My view of politics—and of myself—was changing, but the transformation was not yet complete. Somewhere in all this information overload, I was introduced to Ayn Rand, and I read *The Fountainhead* for the first time. This was *the* pivot point. I discovered that I had much more in common with Howard Roark than with John Kerry or Tom Harkin. And through Howard Roark I suddenly realized how I should be approaching my own career. I realized that I had always been quite self-reliant in the past, but had allowed myself to go down the path of groupthink and liberalism to reinforce my faith in the Democrat Party. I understood that if I was going to work up to my own potential, the only person responsible was me. Most importantly, I wanted the government out of my life to the greatest extent possible.

It's not an easy thing to admit that you've been wrong about something for a long time. I had long accepted the premise that Democrats and liberals were the champions of freedom and of the working class, and that liberalism equaled open-mindedness and compassion. My discovery of libertarianism showed me in black-and-white that nothing could be further from the truth. I asked myself some simple questions. Why did these "champions of freedom" on the Left want to burden us with more and more government regulation? Why were so few of these "defenders of the middle class" actually from working backgrounds, and why was it only okay for *liberals* to be fabulously wealthy? Why were these allegedly open-minded liberals so rigidly partisan? And how was it possible for these loving, compassionate left-wingers to say such vicious, hateful things about those with whom they disagreed politically?

It is fairly common knowledge that the arts are dominated by leftists. What continues to baffle me is that more people in my line of work do not embrace libertarianism! Are not artists supposed to be the ultimate in individualism? Strange then that so many would follow the tenets of collectivism. More specifically, artists should openly embrace free market capitalism and economic liberty; it only makes sense. We want to create a product with the hope that someone will want to buy it, and maybe even want more like it. It doesn't get any more free-market than that! Moreover, the arts are a discretionary expenditure; something a person chooses to spend his or her disposable income on. People enjoy the arts, and the more people out there with disposable income to spend on them, the better things are for all of us in the art world. So economic liberty is a concept which all artists should enthusiastically support. Unfortunately, many modern artists regard capitalism as a great evil, some even going so far as to scorn financial success via one's artwork as "selling out". Very few people with such attitudes stand much chance of success anyway.

Speaking of attitudes, mine changing for the better has been another fabulous by-product of my liberal-to-libertarian trip. As a liberal, I was often bitter and could not deal with life's little inconveniences. As a libertarian, I'm generally happy and optimistic, and can handle anything—come what may. My only regret is not doing this sooner!

Scott Bailiff
Firefighter; Chattanooga, TN

I grew up in a mid-sized town located in southeast Tennessee, Chattanooga. I attended public school and found myself bored and opted to obtain my GED and start a career in 1997. My father ran an insurance settlement company in Atlanta where I got a job. I quickly learned the insurance industry and attending community college. At that time business was booming, so college didn't last long. After September 11, 2001, business abruptly changed. After the towers fell the company's investors, on which we heavily relied, began to retreat.

I returned home in 2001 to find myself broke and unemployed. I took odd jobs, slowly working my way back toward independence and landed a position in California essentially picking up where I left off in the insurance business. But, as the investors continued to retreat and the economy came to crawl, life in the insurance business crumbled. In 2003, I found myself back in Chattanooga at square one. I applied for a job with the fire department and, in 2004, after passing multiple screening tests my dreams came true. I became a firefighter. In 2008 I met Allison, the woman that would change my life forever, and in 2009, I was married with one child on the way.

I am still with the City of Chattanooga and now have a wife and two children. I enjoy my job and family. Because of concern for my children I feel it is important to fight for what is right–our country's founding principles shouldn't be forgotten.

Firefighter Leaves Liberalism
by
Scott Bailiff

For years, I tried loyally to align myself with the Left, as our family dynamic is an openly diverse bunch. Most of my family leans toward the Left and overwhelmingly supports and votes for Democratic Party candidates. The Left seemed more apt to support us and appeared to be the so-called "lesser" of two evils, with the idea that a progressive Democratic Party moves society forward as a whole for the betterment of the populace. Obviously, with me young and all knowing, it would be sometime later before I would come to realize the falsehood of this implication.

The "Lesser" of Two Evils

As you read the title of this essay, it is easy to understand how a young individual at the ripe age of eighteen may come to choose his political preference, and I was no exception. Growing up the only interest I took in the ever-increasing sport of deceit, what I call politics, was listening to my folks, among others, complain about one thing or another only to ultimately repeat the complaint process every so often and never getting anywhere. Everyone talking in circles always amused me. I just didn't get it. I thought this could not be right, this is America and we can change things. We can vote!

However, once I became of age to participate in matters of government, the first step was to choose a party that fit my interests as far as economic and social issues go. What drew me to the Left were mainly social issues. The Democratic Party appeared to be more accepting of diversity and I felt the idea of helping the unfortunate through redistributing wealth seemed like common sense.

Then, I got a job as a firefighter. Not just a desk job working nine to five only worrying about what's in front of me, but a public service job that makes you worry about everything around you as well as the direction you or we, I should say, are headed. Public service work is how you find where the rubber meets the road concerning political issues. For instance, during the winter at our house we usually keep the heat around sixty-eight degrees to conserve energy and save money. However, one cold day at work we received a call to a residence about a disturbance that turned into a medical incident. This residence was a location known to house people that make use of our government's welfare system. Upon entering the home, I could not help but notice how hot it was inside. After commenting on how high their electric bill must be to my co-workers, I received a round of laughter as I was informed that all the buildings in the complex are without electric meters and that this service is free to the residents. After the shock of it all wore off I thought to myself—here I am working two jobs, living paycheck-to-paycheck, doing my best to conserve energy and money to better my family and me while these "frequent flyers" (a term commonly used by first responders to identify repeat offenders of irresponsible use of emergency services) are without any care in the world. I mean they essentially have everything I have and more. Cars, a roof over their head, a running tab with the electric power board, a paycheck, food stamps, no job, no medical costs, and no incentive to change. All set and they do not pay a dime for any of it.

This moment of realization made a huge impact on how I viewed our current system and led me on a path of political discovery that has forever changed my position and attitude about personal responsibility. I began searching for a political platform that looks more closely at following natural law, as our founding fathers did, and encourages people to be more responsible for their own actions. As a result, I found that the Libertarian Party exemplifies these principles by understanding an individual's inalienable rights and the need to protect them from force, fraud, and state conferred privileges that negate them.

Although some in my family may still disagree, it is clear the "lesser" of two evils definition is badly misconstrued. Forward progress is obviously nonexistent with inappropriate nanny state programs paid by coerced taxation. Forward progress can't and won't happen as long as the nanny state remains in place. I can't help but wonder if government dependency for all is the ultimate progressive goal.

As more and more governmental take-overs occur our choices as citizens continue to decrease. This socialistic plan of progression undermines the Constitution our founding fathers created. By masking this with connotations of moving forward for the betterment of all with false advertising is cunning. However, the lies can be uncovered by doing work in the trenches and seeing these programs in action.

The Umbrella Effect

Today, whether the rain trickles up or trickles down the ideology is that our government's job is to supply an umbrella for everyone— the nanny state. This ideology presents a clear and present danger and we all must look closely at the consequences of this type of thinking. As I continued my persistent decision of trying to fit in with the Left, I would habitually justify one flaw with a benefit, another flaw with a benefit, and so on. Until, finally, I found myself alone unable to see the light. The umbrella has gotten so big that it blocks out any sense of hope. With my back broken from carrying the weight, and as the dependents continually multiply, I feel my choices on the progressive path are extremely limited if not null. And I don't see it stopping with conservatism, but only with real policy change.

With both major parties supporting nanny state policies, such as the bailout, checks and balances are thrown to the wayside and agendas are done without due regard for the people. For example, if one wants to stay dry in the rain and be free to roam, one must have an umbrella. If more than one wants to stay dry in the rain and be free to roam, each must have an umbrella. Though this way requires that all rely on themselves to make or buy their umbrella, it allows everyone to go wherever and whenever they want—retaining their inalienable right to liberty. Otherwise, the umbrella needs to be big enough to cover the entire lot and grow with each new addition. And with the government supplying the cover, though we may not have to fend for ourselves, we must go as a group willingly or unwillingly. Thus, our right to choose is grossly taken away and both major parties support this way of thinking. Stripping away people's right to life, liberty, and property for the sake of charity by coercion while removing any remnants of the religious role in our civilized republic goes against this nation's very foundation.

The result is, higher crime rates, lower education standards, fiscal irresponsibility, endless wars, diminishing middle class, corporate mutiny, unemployment hikes, low production and exports, bailouts, recession, and the list goes on and on.

Summary

As we continue this downward spiral and as party lines become more blurred, the idea engrained in the minds of younger generations is the notion that this was not the plan of our founding fathers when they wrote the Constitution of the United States. Without action the so-called "two party system" will lead us, as well as future generations, into something too big to disassemble and eventually running itself without our consent.

Keith Barned
Public School Teacher; Bath, NY

I am a ten-year veteran in the public school system where I work as a special education teacher, and I have done so for all of my years of service. I am married with one son. I will try my hardest to counteract the indoctrination he will no doubt receive as a student in the school system.

A Libertarian Among Leftists
by
Keith Barned

Growing up in upstate New York means that it is almost inevitable that one is going to identify with the political Left, if one isn't entirely apolitical, that is. That is how I spent the better portion of my life before college opened my eyes to the fact that there is more than one side to the politics. They say that there are three sides to every story: yours, theirs, and the truth. It's the same with politics. Unfortunately with politics, the truth is often difficult to find. Everyone has an opinion, and they are never hesitant to share those opinions and call them Truth. We are supposed to think critically and weigh everything others say and decide for ourselves if there is any merit in what they say. However, the educational system of the United States is no longer preparing future generations of citizens to think critically. The public education system is firmly in the hands of the Left, and they are not letting go. Ironically, it was when I was in a teacher preparation program at college that I began to see this, and I was determined to not get blindly caught up in the system.

I grew up in a family that was apolitical at best. My parents rarely talked about politics except to complain about taxes and such. I didn't even know how my parents voted except for the fact that they twice voted for Ronald Reagan. They didn't talk about it or bring us in the voting booth to see how the process worked. I guess they took the "secret ballot" thing to heart. I'm also a product of the public education system in New York State. The only positive thing I can say about it is that when I was going through the ranks, there was actual rigor to the work. We were held accountable for our behavior and effort (or lack thereof). Actions had consequences, and most of us learned from our mistakes. Things have changed since I was a student, and I see the differences clearly since I am now on the other side of the grade book. As a special education teacher, I can see how far things have fallen and how public school has become an extension of the state. It is no longer a place for preparing the next generation to become productive and contributing members of society. Children are no longer held accountable for their actions: Didn't do homework? No problem, you can turn it in later, or not at all. You can't add in your head? Here's a calculator. You don't want to write an essay? Draw me a picture of how you're feeling instead. Outsiders wouldn't believe how easy we make things for students anymore. Calculators are allowed in elementary school. We relax spelling and grammar standards. Cell phones, computers, tablets, all manner of technology are allowed in classrooms to "prepare students for the 21st century world of work." Unfortunately, we have become a service society, and the high tech jobs are no longer available in this country. All we are doing is facilitating a slacker culture.

I grew up left to my own devices. As a middle child, I was left alone as long as I didn't come home in the back of a police car. I saw what I perceived to be "injustice" in the world, and I wondered where the government was to make things better. After all, I reasoned from my lofty teenaged experience, what was government for but to take care of the people? We were lower middle class, and we always had enough, but we never had the extras that many of my friends had, and I thought that it was a bit unfair. Didn't we qualify for food stamps or something, so some of my parents' income was freed up to buy us designer clothes and new bicycles every other year? (It turns out that we probably did qualify.) Because I had no real guidance about politics from my parents, I turned to the other important institution in my life: school. Even then, while the rigor was more than it is now, the liberal mindset dominated in public school, and I got caught up in it. So much so that at the age of ten, I decided that religion was a bunch of baloney, and I told my parents that I didn't believe in God anymore. I refused to go to church, and I actually made my mother cry. We were taught in school that religion was essentially superstition and science was the answer to life's questions. We were taught about the major religions, but it was science that was important.

I went through my teenage years identifying with the Left, and carried that though to a succession of colleges: art school, community college, and two state universities. It was at my final stop in the chain of undergraduate schools, when I finally decided to join the Left as a teacher, that I realized that it was time to think about my political beliefs. While I *identified* with the Left, I never really became a Democrat, liberal, call it what you will. I was registered as an

34

Independent, but I voted Democrat more often than not. I would vote the other side if I thought that their candidate was more in line with my ideals. That all changed when I was in my mid-20s and attending college to become a teacher. Like many people in this country, I had to reevaluate my thinking on September 11, 2001. Classes were cancelled that day, I suspect so the professors could watch the non-stop coverage on cable TV. When things got back to a semblance of normalcy some time later, I was in a required Humanities class, with a visiting professor from South America who was a self-professed "feminist-Marxist." She had a lot to say about how America deserved what happened on that day, and how America's system needed to be brought asunder. It was in that class, with that professor, that I realized what I was getting myself into once I became a teacher—that people on the Left shared more with this professor to one degree or another than I did. At that point, I think I decided to sink into apathy about all things political and just vote the issues.

Unfortunately, that time period was when America started to become more polarized politically. Right versus Left. Conservative versus liberal. Yankees versus Red Sox. Great taste or less filling. It was coming to the point that one had to choose a side or else. I stayed on the sidelines and was blissfully ignorant.

When I finally got out of college and into the classroom as a newly minted teacher, it would have been only too easy to sink back into the warm and fuzzy kumbaya embrace of the liberal Left. In fact, I think it was almost required, due to having to join the teacher's union. Required, because even if one didn't want to join, one still had to pay dues. I began to see exactly how badly public education was preparing our youth for anything but a service job. Requirements were eased; standards were lowered; teachers were teaching to the middle and ignoring those who had more ability because Gifted and Talented programs were all but extinct; and mainstreaming students with disabilities into the regular classroom simply because of the "Free and Appropriate Public Education" section under the Individuals with Disabilities Education Act (IDEA). As a special education teacher myself, I know that certain classified students can be successful in the regular education classroom with minimal supports. However, when students are required to have heavily modified curriculum that is

35

significantly different from their non-disabled peers, as well as specialized equipment, additional personnel supports, etc., it becomes a sideshow.

Heaven forefend that a child should receive instruction outside the regular classroom. Heaven forefend that we recognize that not all students are academically inclined and would do better in a vocational training program. We might actually be able to bring back some of the manufacturing industry if there were enough people with the right type of training. It is all about fairness to the Left in education. Is it fair that one student is exceptionally bright, while there are these others who struggle? Do we need to make the curriculum accessible to all so that the students who are weaker feel a sense of accomplishment? Just like giving out trophies to every kid in a Little League Baseball program, whether they won anything or not. We can't have kids feeling left out!

At this point I started getting interested in politics again. I talked to people, read a lot of books and journal articles, and started to pay attention. The information is out there, but most people can't be bothered to look for it. The more I read, the more disenchanted I became with the Left. I moved towards the middle and decided to straddle the fence. But as one of my colleagues tells students, it can be pretty painful if you straddle the fence and lose your balance. Fence-sitting isn't really my cup of tea, however, so I went completely to the Right, and while I was still registered as an Independent, I began voting party line Republican. It seemed to me that the more Democrats we could replace with good, patriotic Republicans in offices from the local levels all the way up to the top, the better. Republicans cared more for America as a whole than the Democrats did. Or so I thought.

I'm at least as frustrated with the GOP as I am with the Democrats. I started looking for an alternative, and that is when a good friend of mine introduced me to the Libertarian Party. From what I have read, it seems like the Libertarians are genuinely concerned with protecting individual liberty, freedom, and a free market economy. I can identify with that. I have a few issues with libertarian stances on some social issues. I am still a little too socially conservative to completely embrace the Libertarian Party, but I still agree with much of their philosophy.

I know that this essay might sound like I'm biting the hand that feeds me (and my family) by bashing the education system, but nearly every teacher would agree that there is something rotten in the State of Education, to paraphrase *Macbeth*. It doesn't matter which end of the political spectrum teachers fall, we all know that something is broken and needs to be fixed. The differences are in the methods that one believes those fixes should come. Given a different system, I would still love teaching. I do enjoy the interactions with the students, and on those rare occasions when a student makes a connection, it is exciting to see the spark flare, even if it is just for an instant. I still think that there is some good in the system: charter schools and parochial schools in particular. Any school which is not under the heavy hand of the state has a much better chance of turning out the type of productive member of society that this country needs to get back on track. I think that the educational system can still be saved, but it will take a group of strong-willed individuals to stand up to the teachers unions and tell them that enough is enough. It is time to get back to local control of the school systems in this country.

I left the Left completely. One of the most important events in my transition from Left to Right (or wherever I fall now on the political spectrum) was reading Ayn Rand's *Atlas Shrugged*. This novel was an almost religious experience, which is ironic, considering that Rand rejects religion for reason. This is where I break with Rand, because I believe to be well-rounded, a person needs some sort of spiritual belief as well as a solid ability to reason things through. Therefore, I have come back to a spiritual life, I've embraced my Second Amendment rights (the Left would read that as, "This guy is a gun nut"), I have a more solid understanding of Austrian versus Keynesian economics, and I value individual liberty above all else. I've again embraced the ideals of the individual and exceptionalism. I reject every liberal tenet that I once identified with. I also realize that Democrats and Republicans are the pretty much the same, but one party goes a little slower than the other when it comes to destroying traditional American ideals and values. Ironically, I live in one of the most liberal of the several states and I work in the most liberal profession, but in all other matters, I have left the Left.

John A. Charles, Jr.
President and Chief Executive Officer,
Cascade Policy Institute; Portland , OR

John A. Charles, Jr. is president and Chief Executive Officer (CEO) of Cascade Policy Institute, Oregon's free market think tank. John is a frequent keynote speaker and has made presentations in 27 states. He has been published in *The Oregonian, The Pittsburgh Times-Review, The Seattle Times, The Hartford Courant,* and many other outlets. He has also been featured on the "Hannity & Colmes" show, the "Jim Lehrer News Hour", and the cable television hit "Bullshit!" by Penn and Teller.

A native of Pittsburgh, John grew up in New Jersey and moved to Portland in 1980. He has long been active in the community, including stints as a Boy Scout leader, foster parent, reading tutor, and non-profit board member. John is an outdoor enthusiast who enjoys whitewater rafting, hiking, and competitive volleyball.

Why We Left the Left

No Limits to Growth
by
John A. Charles, Jr.

Northern New Jersey was a good place to become an environmental activist in the 1960s. The industrial cities of Perth Amboy, Linden, Rahway, Elizabeth, Newark, and Secaucus hosted vast numbers of oil refineries, chemical plants, junk yards, truck terminals, and tank farms. They were also connected by the 16-lane New Jersey Turnpike, designed with all the aesthetics of a military operation. The air pollution did make for some colorful sunsets, but it was alienating for a nature lover.

I grew up near these eyesores but not among them. Actually, my home town of Cranford was a delightful community of tree-lined streets, single-family homes, and a comfortable downtown. We had plenty of open space and some great parks. Many professionals commuted to New York City for work, but there were also nearby office parks that were job centers.

I developed a strong interest in the natural environment through Boy Scouts. I loved the monthly camping trips and the two weeks we'd spend at Camp Winnebago each summer. Once each year we did a cleanup of the Rahway River, which meandered through the town. Older Scouts used canoes and the younger ones walked the shoreline picking up litter, old shopping carts, tires, and other trash. I was a leader in my troop and proud to be part of these clean-ups.

In the summer after tenth grade my parents paid for me to go on a two-week backpacking trip at the Philmont Scout Reservation in New Mexico, as a reward for earning my Eagle Scout badge. That was by far the most rigorous backcountry experience I ever had, and it really increased my commitment to environmental preservation.

My grandfather also owned 20 acres of woodlands and a small hunting cabin in northwestern Pennsylvania, and my family spent many happy days visiting there. We took long walks, watched the deer graze, and then built a big fire at night. Not everyone in my seven-person family appreciated the "rustic" sleeping accommodations, but I loved it. For many years this was my getaway from the noise and pace of modern America.

In the summer after high school graduation, I discovered a volunteer-based recycling center in Cranford and helped out there on weekends. I found this quite empowering, to be actually doing something to "save the environment." While toiling together in the sun we discussed the problems of bi-metal cans used by large beer companies, which were difficult if not impossible to recycle. Other more senior members described their futile correspondence with Anheuser-Busch on the subject, and this struck me as a more serious form of activism for which I was not quite ready.

In 1972 I enrolled at the University of Pittsburgh, where the marching band was my main social activity. My freshman year was quite liberating, being 400 miles from home and living in the dorms, but I did not get involved in the political aspects of environmental policy or in politics generally. In fact, early in my freshman year I had to take a survey, and one of the questions asked me to place myself on the political spectrum in terms of my beliefs—left, right, or center. I actually skipped the question because I did not understand it.

I was focused simply on surviving the challenges of my freshman year. I wanted to do well in band, study hard, make some friends, meet cute girls, and play intramural sports. I was not involved in the anti-war movement, and the "Watergate" issue to me was just something in the newspaper headlines.

In my sophomore year I began to branch out. A sign was posted seeking members for a new "Science Biology" Club (or something to that effect) that was to be formed. I went to the first meeting, and after a fair amount of discussion of goals and many more meetings, we created the first-ever newspaper recycling program on the Pitt campus. It was rather labor-intensive, but I really enjoyed doing something "hands-on" to conserve resources. It wasn't confrontational or political; it was just a way of offering a new choice to students and creating value out of a waste product.

Also, I took an economics seminar that year where I first learned about "environmental externalities" such as pollution and why we should seek to "internalize" them. That was a powerful concept and helped me think about environmental issues in more political terms.

At roughly the same time I also read the book, *Limits to Growth,* which was based on a series of computer simulations that some MIT academics had run, purporting to show that if consumption trends did not change, the world would run out of important commodities such as copper and oil within 20-30 years. Along with other popular "doomsday" literature such as *The Population Bomb* by Stanford biologist Paul Ehrlich, I became convinced that capitalism was an economic system based on "exponential growth," and with a finite earth, unrestrained growth clearly would not be possible.

I perceived capitalism to be a failed system that needed to be replaced by some form of central planning, since government functionaries certainly would be wise enough to know how to reduce pollution AND they would never be corrupted by anything as crass as money. Not knowing any of them personally, I imagined these central planners to be technical experts who would have no political agenda and simply would devise ways to provide the goods and services in a sustainable fashion.

I remember discussing this with my older sister Claudia one night while we were doing the dishes, and I flatly declared that capitalism was a "dead horse."

My junior year I enrolled in a course offered (for the first time at Pitt) on environmental politics, taught by prominent American historian Samuel P. Hayes. That was the first time I began thinking about environmental issues in a systematic way within a political context. By the end of the term, I was highly motivated to become an environmental activist.

Professor Hayes was a leader in the local Sierra Club chapter, so with his encouragement I began going to meetings. He was also chair of a Club committee on political action, and I joined that as well. We had monthly meetings at his house where we talked about issues and how to use the Sierra Club membership to accomplish political goals. This was a big step for me and it was very exciting to be involved with people who read serious papers, testified in Harrisburg, and were leading the fight to clean up Pittsburgh.

At this point I was in my "experimentation" phase of political philosophy. Among other things, I enrolled in a history class on Marxist thought. I was impressed that the professor claimed to have read every word Karl Marx had ever written. This seemed far beyond anything I could ever do. I never really got anything useful out of the class, but I felt like a real intellectual for taking it.

I also started going to meetings of the local Socialist Workers Party (SWP) and took out a subscription to *The Militant,* a socialist newsweekly closely tied to the SWP. When I returned home for summer and was forced to change the subscription address, it was somewhat embarrassing to have the paper delivered to my suburban home where my parents were no doubt aghast that I was subscribing to a left-wing rag that was probably going to get me on some FBI watch list. But they were wise enough to stay silent (most of the time) and let me feel my way.

At the same time I was beginning to embrace socialism at the theoretical level, I was actually experiencing it in my summer employment. Every summer during my college years, I worked for the Union County Mosquito Control Commission as a laborer. I initially got the job because the mother of one of my high school friends worked in the front office, and she assured me that since they routinely hired about 30 college kids each summer, I would have an excellent chance of getting hired.

The ostensible mission of the Mosquito Control Commission was to reduce the public health and safety problems associated with mosquitoes, which are vectors for malaria and encephalitis. As a practical matter, the day-to-day goal of the Commission was to keep the mosquito population down enough to prevent suburban residents from complaining about bugs annoying them on their back decks or near their swimming pools. The agency was no longer using DDT, and the primary control strategy was to limit the amount of stagnant water available as breeding grounds for mosquitoes. Sometimes this involved draining small marshlands or cleaning out ditches with heavy equipment. There were also thousands of possible breeding sites in and around housing developments—clogged storm water drains on streets, flower pots and spare tires in backyards collecting rainwater, and semi-drained backyard pools of families on vacation.

By the time I started at the Commission I had already had quite a few jobs and was used to working hard. I had been a morning newspaper delivery boy for the *Newark Star-Ledger* in ninth grade. I had worked in the back of a bakery with my brother George as a dishwasher, had worked at a McDonald's restaurant with my other brother Andrew, and had worked in two different tool and die shops. I was used to clocking in and clocking out, doing highly repetitive tasks, and being held accountable for my work production.

But when I showed up for my first day at the Mosquito Commission, I found that these qualities were held in contempt by the permanent workers, who were all members of a public employee union. I was quickly schooled in the Mosquito Commission culture of taking long breakfasts at local diners after leaving the main yard, hanging out in remote hiding spots in the county, and pretending to do work if a supervisor dropped by. Some of the guys also spent time looking for copper wire or other valuables that might be at some curbside, then taking it to a junkyard for cash—on company time.

Most of the college kids wanted to work; we found it incredibly boring to be stuck in a pick-up truck in 95-degree heat trying to kill time. Unfortunately, the dysfunctional culture of the Mosquito Commission was well entrenched, and some of the permanent workers were large men who had quick tempers. I didn't see it as my role to try and reform a corrupt municipal patronage system, especially when my friend's mom worked in the front office.

While at the time I didn't realize it, this was in fact a scale model of the centrally planned society I was dreaming about. It didn't matter that the Mosquito Commission had a noble mission rooted in public health. A politically run commission, overseeing unionized public employees in tasks that were hard to measure, created the ideal conditions for cronyism. After a while, the system worked fine for everyone making money off of it, while most taxpayers had no clue that the Commission even existed.

Today we know this as the problem of "concentrated benefits, dispersed costs." The direct financial benefits of any publicly-funded enterprise are highly concentrated, so employees and contractors have strong incentives to stay informed and show up at any political event where the status quo might be threatened. The financial costs, however, are widely dispersed, and are so small to any one taxpayer that it would not make sense to learn about the problem (if that were even possible) and take action. Moreover, the reform process likely would be arduous and probably unsuccessful.

It was not until decades later that I would come to understand that my experience with the Mosquito Commission was illustrative of why central planning by governmental bureaucracies never works very well.

Meanwhile, as I was about to enter my fourth year at Pitt, I had to make some decisions about my career. I did not see myself working for some large corporation just selling a commodity or service; I wanted to help "save the world." Within the menu of choices available, teaching seemed like the best route. I remember reading *Teaching as a Subversive Activity* by Postman and Weingartner, which had just been published, and I was drawn to that vision.

I enrolled in the School of Education and for student teaching was assigned to teach tenth grade World Cultures at Peabody High School in the East Liberty section of Pittsburgh. I found teaching to be very challenging but rewarding, and looked forward to my career. My general "plan" was to teach for about 20 years while doing environmental activism on the side. Based on my experience in the lunch room with older teachers at Peabody, I figured that after 20 years of teaching I would probably be burned out, and by then I would be able to get a paying job in the environmental movement based on my volunteer work.

September 1977 rolled around and since I hadn't received a teaching offer I took that as a market signal that I would not be employed that fall. At the suggestion of a friend I started job-hunting for positions in other fields, and one day saw an ad in *The New York Times* for a position as administrative assistant for a large environmental organization headquartered in New York City.

I immediately applied and was called for an interview. That's when I discovered that the group was Environmental Defense Fund (EDF), one of the largest and most prestigious environmental activist groups in the nation. EDF had been formed in the late 1960s as an outgrowth of a lawsuit against DDT spraying. At the professional level it was primarily a group of lawyers with some scientists and economists sprinkled in and was not at all like the Sierra Club. There were no local "chapters," and donors were not expected or encouraged to do anything more than send money.

I was interviewed first by the head of direct mail, Madelon Freyman, and then by Executive Director Arlie W. Schardt. The position itself would be primarily working for him, with about 25% of the time dedicated to support in the direct-mail office. I was very enthusiastic and enjoyed the interviews. The following week I stopped in the EDF office. After a minute of sitting in the waiting area, Arlie brought me back to his private office and offered me the job. That was one of the most thrilling moments of my life. I was going to get paid to save the environment, with an office on the 32nd floor of a New York City high rise as well!

Much to my surprise, three weeks later I received a call from a recruiter whom I had met on the Pitt campus the previous year, offering me a fulltime teaching position in a suburban school district just outside Baltimore. Although it was nice to finally get a job offer in the field I had trained for, I turned him down. Working at EDF seemed much more exciting, so that was the end of my teaching career.

The EDF job gave me wonderful insights into the environmental movement because I was working in the national headquarters. The office had the management team, the fundraising staff, accounting, and a mixture of policy staff—a lawyer, an economist, and a scientist. The

Executive Committee of the board also met in New York about six times each year, and I was responsible for planning the logistics of those meetings. I also sat in on all board discussions.

It was at EDF that I began to learn about the strategic need for central control by environmental activists. With a relatively small staff on Manhattan Island and a few branch offices elsewhere, there was no way EDF could affect environmental policy in very many places. So their strategy was to look for legal or regulatory leverage points where focused activity could have far-reaching implications.

Lawyers, of course, look for cases where there is potential for establishing a legal precedent, thus controlling all future legal decisions in that field. But the other staff did the same. They looked for ways to manipulate regulatory bodies such as state public utility commissions or the federal Consumer Product Safety Commission in ways that a key decision would force entire industries to change.

New agencies such as the Environmental Protection Agency (EPA) were perfectly set up to accommodate this approach. As Congress passed more and more environmental laws, increasing amounts of authority were delegated to EPA in the form of notice-and-comment rulemaking. Groups such as EDF and Natural Resources Defense Council (NRDC) monitored federal agencies and submitted extensive comments on proposed rules.

If they successfully shaped the rules in their favor, economic activities in all 50 states would be affected. Decentralized decision-making by individuals operating in dynamic markets could never be controlled by environmental groups in New York or Washington, DC, so those groups needed central decision-making by powerful bureaucracies in order to exert their influence.

I worked at EDF for more than two years, serving as Arlie's executive assistant and answering all mail from the public. I also did some public speaking and media work. My very first television interview (regarding asbestos liners in hand-held hair dryers, where I used several of my sisters' hair dryers as props) was with a local ABC "Eyewitness News" reporter named Joan Lunden. About two weeks after my interview she was named co-host of "Good Morning America," a post she held for over two decades. I always felt I had something to do with her rise to fame.

I loved working for Arlie, but in 1979 he left in a dispute with the board, and my position became precarious. Later that year the board hired Janet W. Brown as the new executive director. She lived in Washington, DC and planned to commute part-time to New York. As she settled in it was clear that I was not part of her plans.

Fortuitously, a friend in the fundraising department took a pregnancy leave of absence and I moved into her position on a temporary basis. That was actually a lucky break in terms of my professional development, as it gave me a first-hand tutorial in dealing with foundations, direct-mail fundraising, and large-gift soliciting. I helped proofread grant applications and took the lead in researching smaller family foundations. I also took night classes at New York University in fundraising and public relations.

I started looking for work elsewhere, preferably in the New York area. However, the Oregon Environmental Council (OEC), based in Portland, was looking for a new executive director in the fall of 1979. Though I was only 25, I applied for the job, knowing that my brief stint at EDF would at least capture the attention of the hiring committee.

After a three-month interview process I was hired, despite knowing little about Oregon. This was a concern to OEC, but a board member, Char Corkran, promised to give me a proper introduction to the fabulous wild places in Oregon and the politics of saving those places. Char and her husband Dave had a 14-year-old son and I went with them on outings to the Oregon coast, the Washington Cascades, Steens Mountain, and various other places. I had dinner at their Portland home many times. Char was a naturalist and long-time activist, and Dave was a history teacher at The Catlin Gabel School, a private school near their home. Between 1980 and 1984, when Char left the OEC Board, they were a huge influence on my life.

OEC was quite different from EDF. The Council was much smaller. The annual budget for 1980 was around $70,000, compared with $1.9 million at EDF. It was not a highly professional organization; it was a grassroots group that maintained a regular lobbying presence in the state capital, Salem. The OEC office was an old Victorian house in a rundown Portland neighborhood. Only one person on the staff had enough money for a car.

It was an exciting time for the environmental movement and for me personally. Since I was single and didn't know anyone in Portland, I threw my whole life into the cause.

In 1981 I began lobbying in the state legislature for the first time, where I learned about the politics of environmental policy-setting. Oregon's part-time, non-professional legislature lent itself well to citizen influence. Without the small armies of aggressive staff members trying to keep people from seeing their boss—characteristic of larger state legislatures or Congress—you could easily meet with elected officials. Over the next decade I helped pass dozens of environmental laws and participated in numerous rule-making proceedings with state agencies. I also served on many advisory committees and task forces, related to issues such as indoor air pollution, field burning, motor vehicle emissions, groundwater, and protection of scenic vistas in the Grand Canyon.

I did not work much on saving wild places—there were many other groups doing that. I worked mostly in the pollution control field. Knowing that I needed to specialize in something in order to be effective, I focused on air quality during the 1980s and then transportation policy during the 1990s.

Organizationally, I helped raise money, hired new staff, and persuaded the board to change the tax status from 501(c)(4) to 501(c)(3), which meant that contributions would be tax deductible to donors. This was a key factor in allowing the organization to grow and to seek foundation grants, because all foundations require recipient organizations to have a tax deductible status. This helped increase the annual budget to over $400,000.

Now that I had permanently left the teaching profession behind, I started taking night classes at local colleges to arm myself with new skills. Eventually I enrolled at Portland State University with the goal of getting a master's degree in public administration. I felt that the curriculum in the MPA program would help me learn about policy analysis, legal issues, personnel management, and public budgeting. This would help me at OEC, and would also lay the groundwork for my next move, which logically pointed in the direction of running a state environmental agency. I entered the program around 1984 on a part-time basis and received my MPA degree in 1991.

For most of the 1980s I also served on the volunteer board of the Oregon League of Conservation Voters (OLCV), the Political Action Committee for the mainstream environmental movement. In that capacity I helped interview legislative candidates, evaluate voting records of all legislators at the conclusion of each session, and allocate money for individual campaigns.

In 1988 I was contacted by a New York activist, Judith Enck, who was interested in holding a conference where people working for the various state environmental "Councils" could meet. Since this was the pre-Internet era, all of us were working in isolation. I thought this was a wonderful idea and agreed to help.

Ms. Enck, who later became a top environmental advisor to Governor Eliot Spitzer, worked with generous donors from The Beldon Fund to draft an agenda. The Fund offered to pay for the travel costs of one person to attend from the various environmental groups. In the fall of that year 19 of us met at a low-cost conference center in Washington, DC for about three days. Meeting leaders from such groups as the Michigan Environmental Council, Montana Environmental Information Center, and the Natural Resources Council of Maine was very empowering.

The State Environmental Leadership Conference (SELC) became an annual event. In 1990 I was in charge of the conference, which was held at a beautiful resort in Colorado. With a fair amount of influence over the agenda, I was able to bring in my former professor and mentor, Sam Hayes, as a guest speaker. It was very satisfying for me to know that during the past 15 years I had evolved from being a shy, non-activist student at the University of Pittsburgh to becoming a state environmental leader helping to form a national network.

After eight years of working at OEC I received the Richard E. Neuberger award, the highest award given by the Council. I received the award at our annual dinner that year, and I had no idea this was going to happen. Of course I was honored, but I was also honored that Del Langbauer of the Harder Foundation joined us that evening to announce that we had been selected to receive a three-year challenge grant to create an endowment.

The Harder Foundation had been supporting us since 1979, and had come to recognize that advocacy organizations needed two things from private foundations: general support grants and endowment grants. We were the second group to receive an endowment grant from the Harder Foundation, which was quite an honor. The terms of the challenge were that we had to raise certain amounts of money for the endowment over a three-year period, and if we did so, they would match it dollar-for-dollar and then issue us a bonus fourth year.

To create an endowment fund was a sign of organizational maturity, so I was very proud that the Harder Foundation had selected us. Moreover, the Foundation thought enough of my management that one of the stipulations of the grant contract was that I write a how-to manual on running a state-based environmental lobbying organization. This was a daunting task and I didn't necessarily feel qualified to write it. But over the next several years I worked on it and also interviewed colleagues at annual SELC conferences to get their perspectives. I eventually published the booklet in 1995 and the Harder Foundation distributed to all of their grantees and other interested organizations.

By the early 1990s OEC was strong, and many of the board members had become close friends of mine. The future looked bright both personally and professionally. But my political views were evolving, and this would eventually cause a conflict. It appeared to me that the traditional command-and-control strategies of the 1970s— complicated federal statutes administered by large bureaucracies based in Washington, DC—were reaching the point of diminishing marginal returns. As total pollution levels continued to drop, it became more and more difficult to address the last increments through these statutory programs.

Also, I began noticing the rise of a new approach—known as Free-Market Environmentalism (FME). Pioneered primarily by some academics in Bozeman, Montana who had formed the Foundation for Research on Economics and the Environment (FREE) and the Political Economy Research Center (PERC), FME promoted the idea that we could achieve better environmental outcomes through decentralized decision-making and the strict enforcement of property rights, operating within a dynamic market economy. I received several complimentary books in the mail on the subject from PERC and the Pacific Research Institute (PRI) in San Francisco, and these books influenced my thinking.

In 1990 OEC was planning a board/staff-member retreat and one of the panel discussions was supposed to be about market-based approaches to traffic and motor vehicle emissions. A group in San Francisco called the Bay Area Economic Forum (BAEF) had done some very innovative work promoting a package of incentive-oriented policies such as emissions fees and peak-hour road pricing. I called to see if the staff director would be available to speak at our retreat. He said he could, but a few weeks later he had to cancel.

He gave me three names of people who might be able to substitute. I called the first two and was turned down. I made my last call to an economist named Randy Pozdena, who worked at the Federal Research Bank of San Francisco. Not only was he available, he said the bank would pick up the tab for his trip. I was told that he had written much of the policy material of the BAEF, so I was looking forward to his presentation.

His speech at the retreat focused on the use of so-called "congestion pricing" as a mechanism for minimizing or eliminating highway traffic jams. He had a short slide show, but the slides were visually powerful. One in particular showed that the cost of providing highway capacity to drivers varied by a huge margin depending on the time of day, day of the week, and direction of travel—yet the standard mechanism for paying for roads, the gas tax, was fixed. He mentioned that it was now possible to collect real-time user fees by motorists via transponders placed in the windshields of cars, and thus road user fees could be varied to reflect the variable costs. The benefits of doing so would be to reduce peak-hour traffic and improve highway travel speeds.

This immediately struck me as a powerful concept, and I felt that I needed to learn more about it. I had been vaguely familiar with congestion pricing because the "intellectual leader" of the congestion pricing movement was William Vickery, a Columbia University economist who had once visited the EDF office. Although elegant in theory, the problem with congestion pricing had always been that tolls needed to be collected manually at toll plazas, which did not reduce congestion, they *increased* it.

However, the advent of commercial transponder technology changed everything. Now tolls could be collected at actual travel speed without the need for any tollgates. I soon learned that the Oklahoma Turnpike Commission had just implemented electronic tolling on its entire statewide system, which demonstrated that it could be done both technologically and politically. I concluded that this was going to be the road finance mechanism of the future.

Randy and I hit it off and kept in touch. Two years later he moved to Portland, and we recruited him to the OEC board. His disciplined thinking about the role of markets in solving environmental problems was extremely helpful to me and made me question standard orthodoxy about environmental policy.

At roughly the same time, a Eugene-based economist, Randal O'Toole, was undergoing a transformation in his thinking about environmental issues and this was affecting me as well. O'Toole had run a small firm called the Cascade Holistic Economic Consultants (CHEC) in the 1970s and '80s, where he had pioneered the use of economic analysis in federal forest planning to show that many of the timber sales on federal lands were not only environmentally destructive, but lost money for federal taxpayers as well. He then wrote a book, *Reforming the Forest Service*, arguing that federal land managers made these decisions because their budgets were controlled by Congress and local United States Forest Service (USFS) managers were incentivized by the budget process to cut timber excessively. Most or all of O'Toole's clients had been small environmental groups during that period, and he was considered something of a hero for his use of quantitative analysis in critiquing USFS forest plans.

But his analysis of federal forest planning led him to look more carefully at the role of *institutional incentives in decision-making*, and he gradually became a strong proponent of FME. I had known of Randal during those years and he frequently sent complimentary copies of his newsletters and papers to OEC. I was watching his evolution and it made me feel like I was moving in the right direction, especially when he put CHEC behind him and started a new home for himself, the Thoreau Institute. His new journal, *Different Drummer*, billed itself as a journal for "libertarian environmentalism," a phrase that I did not even understand. But I read it and learned a great deal about the inherent problems with central planning.

Oregon Land-Use Regulation: Central Planning on Steroids
One of the most iconic "progressive" policies in Oregon is statewide land-use regulation, adopted by the legislature in 1973. This law requires that every square inch of land be zoned by government planners, in accordance with comprehensive plans adopted in strict adherence to 19 statewide planning "goals." The overarching policy goal of the system is to "limit sprawl" (a term not actually defined) and preserve most private, non-urban lands in zoning designations mandating commercial-scale farming and forestry.

When I arrived in Oregon I had no idea how this system worked, and even by the 1990s I was still relatively unfamiliar with it. I relied on land-use planning friends to tell me what made sense. This led to an unexpected result when in October 1992 I received a fax from Henry Richmond, co-founder and executive director of 1000 Friends of Oregon, the state's leading advocate for land-use planning. The fax was an "Action Alert" regarding a land-use planning policy that was being considered by the state Land Conservation and Development Commission (LCDC) on the arcane subject of "secondary lands."

According to the fax, the proposed rules would "fail to protect natural resources such as wildlife habit, groundwater resources, and air quality." Mr. Richmond claimed that such failures would be "perhaps the biggest threat to Oregon's land use program since its inception nearly 20 years ago!"

What struck me as incongruous about the memo was that LCDC was then under the direct control of Governor Barbara Roberts, a liberal Democrat who was as strongly supportive of state land-use planning as any governor in Oregon history. As a state legislator, she had been schooled on these issues by 1000 Friends lobbyists Dick Benner and Bob Stacey.

Mr. Benner was now the head of the Department of Land Conservation and Development—which administered the policies of the LCDC—and the chair of the LCDC was Bill Blosser, who had a graduate degree in planning and was a co-owner of a prominent winery.

From my perspective, this was the "Dream Team" of land-use regulation, yet they were being publicly criticized by the state's leading pro-planning group for proposing the *greatest threat to planning in 20 years!*

My colleagues and planning mentors had always criticized state and local government officials for "caving in" or "selling out" on the issues. As they usually described it, there was nothing wrong with the statewide land-use regulatory system—it's just that the people running it were not good enough to make it work.

But that argument didn't make sense any more. I couldn't see myself writing a letter to Dick Benner accusing him of threatening land-use planning. It was clear to me that if this was the way 1000 Friends would treat their philosophical allies in power, land-use regulation was not suffering from "bad people." It was suffering from a "bad system." Apparently, no one was good enough to run it.

From then on my relations with all of my planner friends began to deteriorate as I started openly challenging their fundamental beliefs.

At roughly the same time, the regional planning authority, Metro, was launching a huge process to draft a 50-year land-use/transportation plan for the region, known as the 2040 Plan. As a prominent environmental leader I was invited to a special briefing over at the Metro headquarters, and some things stated at that briefing raised red flags for me. The planners seemed very arrogant about what they wanted and quite unconcerned about the effects their grand visions would have on people. I heard the term "big-box retail" for the first time at this meeting, and it was clearly spoken as a pejorative.

Up until then, I had simply thought of stores like WalMart as places with really great selection at low prices. But the planners were making it clear that large-format stores were socially undesirable because they had big parking lots in front, parking lots promoted driving, and driving was bad.

Over a period of five to six years a great deal of taxpayer money was spent on the 2040 planning process. Much of it was wasted on a vast "public outreach" campaign designed to create the perception of grass-roots support for policy outcomes that had already been decided. However, not all of it was spent on PR. Metro actually hired some excellent consultants, who told Metro that their grand vision of a tight urban growth boundary, forced reductions in vehicle miles traveled, and huge expenditures on rail transit were likely to have numerous negative side-effects.

One of the consultants to Metro told them in 1996 that the 2040 plan *"incorporates and illustrates many of the impacts that one would expect when one assumes substantial growth and or limited expansion of land supply: reduced average lot sizes, a greater proportion of households in multifamily housing, decreased percentage of households owning their own homes, increased percentage of household income spent on housing, and increased number of housing units that will require subsidy."*[1]

Most of these outcomes were obviously undesirable, and I could not understand why all the local planners and environmental advocates were being supportive of the 2040 Plan. As the Plan went into the public hearing process, I wrote up 16 pages of comments criticizing it.

I shared a draft with the OEC policy committee, which was comprised mostly of land-use lawyers. One member said that the first 12 pages needed to be cut. I pointed out that I was quoting Metro's own consultants, but that did not persuade them. I was challenging the dominant ideology, and that was simply not allowed.

At that moment, I knew that my time with OEC was drawing to a close.

The Metro Council adopted the 2040 Plan in late 1995, with all criticisms duly noted and ignored. It was becoming obvious that the Portland regional planning bureaucracy had become so large and powerful that it was now a self-perpetuating machine, disconnected from public opinion or control.

A year later Randal O'Toole would publish a devastating critique of the 2040 plan that reinforced all my concerns. It was a surprise to me that he was even involved, but unbeknownst to me Randal had moved from Eugene to an old residential community southeast of Portland called Oak Grove. This unincorporated community was characterized by single-family homes with wide streets, little traffic, and large yards. Metro was trying to re-zone the community to fit the 2040 template, whereby the "wasted space" of large back yards would be replaced with four-story apartment complexes and condo bunkers, a slow light rail train would be brought in, and the increased density would generate lots of local traffic.

One of his neighbors slipped a flyer under his doormat inviting him to come to a neighborhood meeting to discuss the problems with the plan. At that point O'Toole knew almost nothing about Metro, Smart Growth, or any other aspect of the whole regional planning agenda. But he quickly learned and didn't like what he saw, so he turned his attention away from federal forest issues to urban planning. Metro had inadvertently woken a sleeping bulldog who would quickly become an international leader in the fight against dysfunctional government planning.

Portland Light Rail: A Solution in Search of a Problem

When I first moved to Portland I was very pro-transit. I had grown up riding buses into New York City, subways to Shea Stadium, and had gone to college on an urban campus where taking buses was normal. Portland's first light rail line opened in 1986, and like many other Portland residents, I eagerly took a short spin on it (since it was free that day). It seemed nice enough, but as a practical matter it didn't go very many places, so even though I was living about one mile north of the rail line, I never rode it because two bus lines were much more convenient.

In fact, the more I spent time learning about the Metro 2040 plan, the more doubts I was having that even a complete light rail system would have much social value. Sometime during the 1995 legislative session I had a conversation in the capitol with a Portland-area state legislator about light rail and expressed to him (in private) my growing concerns that light rail seemed expensive, inflexible, and not useful to most residents. To my surprise, he passed on these comments to someone on my board, and I was asked to attend a meeting with board members so we could discuss this apparent transgression.

Toward the end of the meeting I brought up the issue of light rail over the Columbia River to Vancouver, Washington, which was a popular transit fantasy. I said I didn't really understand why light rail to Vancouver was important, given that we already had express bus service in that corridor. My Board president, a prominent land-use lawyer, patiently explained the rationale from his perspective, showing the straight line of the proposed tracks from Vancouver to Portland.

I responded, "But what if people don't want to travel just in that corridor?" He looked me in the eye and said in total seriousness, "But John, this is where *we want them to go.*"

I was dumbstruck by the comment. It was classic Portland planner language, both arrogant and naïve. The entire 2040 planning process was all about treating people as little chess pieces to be moved around according to planner dictates. Important attributes such as *consumer preference* or *financial feasibility* were largely irrelevant.

Yet despite these concerns about the politics and financing of light rail, in my private life I was about to buy a house based largely on its access to rail. In May 1995, after getting divorced and needing a new place to live with room for my teenage son, I starting looking for a house and searched exclusively on the east side of Portland because I wanted to be a rail commuter again (I had always commuted to the New York EDF office by rail). Portland only had one light rail train at the time, running from downtown to Gresham on the east side. After a few months I bought a small home along the Sandy River in unincorporated Clackamas County.

Beginning June of 1995, my new commute to OEC was to drive 20 miles west to the end of the light rail line in Gresham, park in a free TriMet parking lot, then take rail for 44 minutes to downtown Portland. However, once I became a regular light rail commuter, it became clear that simply thinking about rail was a lot more fun than actually riding it. Unlike my experiences on the east coast with real commuter trains and high-capacity/high-speed express subways in New York, light rail proved to be excruciatingly slow and unpleasant. With a limit of only two cars per train (due to the short blocks in downtown Portland), the trains had very few seats so they quickly became crowded after leaving Gresham in the morning.

This was described by train advocates as "proof" that they were popular, but in fact it just showed that light rail was a low-capacity transit system. Yet to this day TriMet and Metro both refer to light rail as "high-capacity" transit.

After a few months I called TriMet to ask why they did not offer express service, since the name of the train was Metropolitan Area Express (MAX). I was told that the name was suggested by someone in a public contest and chosen because it sounded nice, not because it meant anything. When I pointed out that there were by-pass tracks at Gateway and the Rose Quarter that would allow express trains to pass locals, he simply said that there were no plans to offer premium service.

Not wanting to be argumentative, I asked if there were plans to have express service on the Westside line, which was then under construction. Again he said, "no." I then asked if TriMet intended to offer express trains on any future lines at any time. He patiently replied, "Sir, it's not in our plan."

It reminded me of a Lily Tomlin movie where she declares, "We don't care. We don't have to care—we're the phone company." By now the telephone monopoly was a thing of the past, but TriMet was a municipal transit monopoly, so it had no reason to innovate.

In addition to my growing alienation from the TriMet system, my new residence in a semi-rural part of Clackamas County helped change my thinking about all kinds of environmental and planning issues. I was now living on an isolated road on a one-acre lot, 10 miles from the nearest city. Clackamas County is a large, predominantly rural county, and I began to see that so many of the policies being enacted by the state were driven by the urban agenda of Portland. And the people driving that agenda had very little tolerance for perspectives of those from other parts of the state.

Soon thereafter I had a letter to the editor published in a local liberal weekly on some urban planning topic, and that annoyed certain board members. So one of my long-time friends on the board took me to breakfast and said, "You're losing the board." It was pretty clear that we were growing in different directions and it would soon be time to move on.

Leaving OEC

In 1995 the board hired a mediator to help facilitate the ideological disputes we were having, but that didn't really work. In the early part of 1996 I had a meeting with the board president and one other board member, and it was agreed that I would leave at the beginning of October. At first it was shocking to contemplate that my time there would soon be over, and a few of the "pro-market" board members encouraged me to reconsider. But after crossing the threshold it was actually liberating to examine new possibilities. I helped the board with the executive search while simultaneously looking around for my next progression.

Fortuitously, Cascade Policy Institute (CPI) had incorporated in 1991 as a libertarian think tank and was busy spreading its vision through reports and educational events. For some reason they started sending literature to the OEC office so I gradually became aware of their work. In 1994 CPI sponsored the first of what would become four biennial "Better Government" competitions (BGCs), aimed at soliciting ideas to reduce the scope of government or make it work better. The competition promised that ten winning ideas would be chosen and that the people promoting those ten concepts would be eligible for grants to turn them into business plans for implementation.

In 1994 I submitted congestion pricing as a BGC concept. Although it was not chosen as a winner, it did expose me more to the organization, and I began attending some of the functions. I went to a luncheon featuring José Piñera, the world's leading expert on creating personal accounts within national Social Security systems. I also went to a small seminar with the founder of the charter school movement, Ted Colderie, and I listened to a fairly radical speech by Marshall Fritz, leader of a group called Separation of School and State. All of the ideas being advocated by these speakers were extremely thought provoking and I was very attracted to them.

Toward the end of my OEC tenure I gave a speech at a statewide transportation conference. Afterwards, Kate Deane from the City of Portland said to me, "John, you should go work for Cascade Policy Institute." I responded, "I'm not a libertarian, and besides I don't think they're hiring."

I really did not take the suggestion very seriously, as it seemed like too big of a leap. Yet I was getting to know the folks at Cascade because I submitted another concept for the 1996 Better Government Competition, and this time I was named one of the ten winners. My idea was to sell the state's "common school trust lands," including a large state forest on the southern Oregon coast, and use the money (estimated to be close to $1 billion) to fund a school voucher program. The Oregon "trust lands" are lands that were deeded to the state by the federal government upon statehood, for the purpose of generating revenue to help support the "common schools."

Unfortunately, under state management, the lands make very little money, so in 1995 the managing agency proposed in a draft report that the entire portfolio of forest lands and grazing lands be sold off and the money put into stocks and bonds, to be managed by the Oregon Investment Council.

I thought this was a very good idea and supported it, then added the concept of using the cash to help create a voucher program that would add choice and competition to the monopolistic state school system. Ultimately the proposal to sell off state lands was withdrawn due to political opposition, but it did at least create an opportunity to talk about it. Cascade hosted a luncheon in the fall of 1996 to honor the ten BGC winners and it was fun to have my idea recognized in front of a large crowd.

By November 1996 I had left OEC and Randal O'Toole was trying to organize opposition to the Metro 2040 Plan. He contacted me and we me a few times, along with Steve Buckstein of Cascade and others. We were all opposed to the Plan but there was no organization dedicated to stopping it. Randal suggested casually that we form one and that I run it. Apparently, he also mentioned to Steve that Cascade should hire me for the same purpose.

In December Steve called me into the small Cascade office to discuss various issues. This casual conversation turned out to be a job interview; Steve asked if I would be interested in working at CPI fulltime to research and write about FME. I was surprised but accepted the offer and began working for CPI in January 1997.

My move was probably a shocking bit of news to my former colleagues, and a bit shocking to me as well. I knew that this would be the formal divorce from my entire social network of friends, and at first it was difficult to accept. I tried to moderate some of my public statements, but the major media outlets actually played up the change.

For instance, in my first big op-ed that I wrote for *The Oregonian* about why urban growth boundaries don't work, I wasn't all that comfortable with the short bio statement at the end, which listed my affiliation with CPI but also said I had been executive director with OEC for nearly 17 years. I asked the editor if it was really necessary to mention that, and he said, "That's the entire reason

I'm running this piece." Journalists love conflict, so they were not going to soft-sell my change of career.

Gradually, I got over the social discomfort and embraced my new role. Some of my long-time friends were happy for my change and were intellectually curious. With those people, we could discuss issues in a civil manner. A few even moved in the same philosophical direction as me over time. But for most, my change meant that our friendship was over.

At Cascade I focused on a range of environmental issues and studied ways to use property rights, decentralized decision-making, and the dynamic market process to protect environmental quality. Soon after taking the job, the "Smart Growth" craze swept the country, and people from all over the country started contacting me about Portland, since politicians in the Portland region had been attempting to implement Smart Growth principles for decades. Being responsive to market demands, I started focusing research and writing on urban transit and growth management issues. Eventually I made hundreds of presentations and traveled to over 27 states to debunk the myths of Portland.

I loved working as an analyst, but in October 2004 the CPI board made several management changes. Steve Buckstein stepped down as CEO to focus on policy analysis, and I was asked to temporarily serve in that role. I agreed, with no particular desire to make it a permanent arrangement. But after spending six months helping the board recruit executive talent and being dissatisfied with what we were finding, we mutually came to the decision in April 2005 that I would remain in the position permanently.

Why Change?
People frequently ask me why I spent 20 years of my life in the mainstream environmental movement and then went to work for a libertarian think tank. There is no single reason, nor was there any one moment when my worldview changed. It was just a steady evolution spurred by events, people, and life experiences.

My early political beliefs started getting trumped by reality, so I had two basic choices: either change my assumptions, or deny reality. I decided that changing my assumptions would be easier.

Also, as an environmental activist I was closely tracking the doomsday predictions of the 1970s, and they ended up being completely wrong. Most pollution trends were heading in the right direction even when *Limits to Growth* was published, and by the 1990s it was obvious that total ambient levels of emissions were steadily dropping even though population, miles of motorized driving, and the number of business enterprises were growing. This has been a fantastic achievement and can only be explained by the technological innovation and wealth creation fostered by capitalism.

Eventually I came to be familiar with the work of the late economist Julian Simon, who dedicated the bulk of his career to showing that the doomsday predictions would always be wrong and that the earth would never run out of resources because human ingenuity was the "ultimate resource." In fact, Simon made a famous bet with Paul Ehrlich that over a ten-year period, a basket of ten commodities would decline in price, demonstrating abundance, not scarcity. Simon won the bet and Ehrlich had to pay up (with winnings going to charity).

After the Soviet Union collapsed and the Berlin Wall was taken down, it became obvious that the most polluted and dangerous places on earth were those that had been largely under central control of government for a very long time. Although there may be such things as "market failure" which can result in pollution, it's very clear that "government failure" is ubiquitous and almost impossible to overcome.

In a market economy, profit-seeking companies fail all the time and are forced to write off losses or even declare bankruptcy. This is an inevitable part of the "creative destruction" of the marketplace, necessary so that capital can be reallocated to higher purposes.

Elected officials rarely engage in creative destruction of failed programs because they don't have to. In fact, policy failure is usually rewarded with more money and more power. Thus, vast societal resources are wasted decade after decade even when programs no longer serve a purpose (if they ever did).

The amount of information that politicians or agency managers try to gather for their regulatory plans—for environmental protection, education, health care, or any other sector of the economy—is so vast that it cannot be processed, and even if it could, most of it would quickly be out of date. Only a dynamic market economy responding instantaneously to billions of price signals, dreams, hunches, and consumer decisions can bring forth the goods and services we desire at a cost we can afford.

After 35 years in the trenches of public policy decision-making, it's clear that central planning doesn't work and we should stop trying to make it work. Living in Portland has given me a front-row seat to the absurdities of taking this paradigm to its logical conclusion. Under the direction of local politicians, bureaucrats and environmental activists, Portland has become something of a central planning circus act. It is now even the subject of a parody television show, *Portlandia*, which mocks the political correctness of intrusive government.

There is no shame in admitting that a political philosophy that once seemed appealing is wrong. The only shame is in making the same mistakes over and over again. The problem with advocates of central control is that they never own up to their mistakes, because they don't have to. Monopoly power has its privileges.

Our challenge now is to take back that power and disperse it to where it should reside, with the people.

End Notes
1.   Hobson Johnson & Associates. *Working Paper: Residential Market Evaluation, 2040 Means Business Committee.* November 1996.

Gary Chartier
Associate Dean of the School of Business
And Associate Professor of Law and
Business Ethics at La Sierra University; Riverside, CA

Gary Chartier is Associate Dean of the School of Business and Associate Professor of Law and Business Ethics at La Sierra University. He holds a PhD from the University of Cambridge and a JD from the University of California, Los Angeles. He is the author of three books—*The Conscience of an Anarchist, Economic Justice and Natural Law*, and *The Analogy of Love*—and of articles in scholarly journals including the *Oxford Journal of Legal Studies*, *Legal Theory*, and the *Canadian Journal of Law and Jurisprudence*, as well as the co-editor of another, *Markets Not Capitalism: Individualist Anarchism against Bosses, Inequality, Corporate Power, and Structural Poverty.* A member of the Alliance of the Libertarian Left, he serves as a member of the advisory panel for the Center for a Stateless Society, and as a member of the editorial board of *Libertarian Papers*.

There and Back Again
by
Gary Chartier

A libertarian in high school and college, I became a leftist in my early twenties—and assumed that this meant I also needed to embrace the state. I cast one vote for Bill Clinton (for whom I also campaigned), one for Socialist David Cobb, and three for Ralph Nader, and I published scholarly articles presupposing the desirability of solving social problems using state power. But as George W. Bush and Barack Obama helped me to abandon statism, I discovered that I could remain an authentic leftist while returning to libertarianism.

I

I was riding in the back seat of an enormous, old, green Cadillac, part of a group of half a dozen friends. Well, five friends, and Amandine. She was in front, holding forth.

She was lovely, intelligent, spirited—and, as far as I could see, an utterly humorless zealot. She'd been where I was, she let me know, and my adolescent naïveté wouldn't last. "Full-fledged libertarian at fifteen? Full-fledged socialist at nineteen!" she announced.

I didn't enjoy the needling. A little later in the conversation, I had fun feigning enthusiasm for Hitler just so I could see Amandine whirl around in angry shock before realizing she was being mocked. She retreated into silence.

What's ironic, though, is that she turned out to be right. I was probably closer to twenty-one than to nineteen when I made the transition, but I would certainly have called myself a socialist well before I was thirty. What's also ironic is that I still would; except that I'm also a libertarian again.

II

Born in Glendale, California, in 1966, I was in many ways typical of budding libertarians of my generation. My parents were Taft and then Goldwater Republicans.[1] I liked computers. I read science fiction. I was socially awkward. I read Murray Rothbard, Friedrich

66

Hayek (whom I proclaimed "my favorite economist"), Robert Nozick, Milton and Rose Friedman, and Robert Anton Wilson with enthusiasm. I reached out to the wider libertarian world by ordering freedom-oriented books from a mail-order catalogue printed in tiny type. I discovered the Libertarian Party (moving house recently, I chanced on flyers for the 1980 Ed Clark campaign). And finding my way onto a libertarian mailing list resulted in my receiving a 1984 form letter—something I also rediscovered recently—from Ron Paul asking that I support the fledgling Mises Institute.

Nozick was a great intellectual work-out, though by far the most difficult author I'd ever tried to read. But Rothbard affected me much more profoundly: looking back on my thinking in late adolescence, I'm struck by how much I imbibed from him, even as I disagreed with him about various things. When I returned to libertarianism, thinking like a Rothbardian sometimes (not always) seemed like slipping on an old, familiar shoe.

My libertarianism was a product of a visceral anti-authoritarianism (perhaps fed by my relationship with a domineering father—who himself had little time for arbitrary authority) and of my attempts to take my parents' political convictions to their logical conclusions (my own peculiar form of adolescent rebellion). One of the most passionate arguments I remember having with my dad during my teenage years involved zoning laws, which I despised and he defended, despite his passionate attachment to property rights. Similarly: I wrote an essay called "Redistribution for the Common Good: The Conservative Dilemma," in which I argued that it was inconsistent to oppose tax-funded domestic spending while favoring tax-funded military spending, as he and other Republicans certainly did.

III

As a libertarian, I—rightly—took freedom seriously. But I hadn't thought much, or very seriously, about issues like poverty and systemic injustice.

Amandine changed that.

She had arrived in college a naïve young libertarian who had been overwhelmed by a favorite teacher's depiction of an unjust world. I now believe that she could have shared his passion for justice and his disgust at oppression while retaining her libertarian beliefs; but she lacked the set of ideas and tools she would have needed to do so, and, concluding that the choice was between caring about the poor and the oppressed and continuing to endorse an ideology that didn't seem designed for the real world, she abandoned her libertarian views.

While my first reaction to her was a mixture of fear (what if she was right that I was doomed to be a socialist?) and anger, a year later, when she returned after studying in Europe, I found myself smitten with her. (Nothing came of my crush.) I tried in good faith to enter into her perspective, attempting in particular to share her concern with feudal injustice south of the border. I even wrote a substantial short story for her—about a wealthy young man who returns to his home in Latin America and becomes involved in opposing his violent older brother, who is actively repressing discontented peasants.

IV

Despite my crush on a state socialist, I was certainly still a libertarian when, a year later, I received my high-school diploma and began full-time college study. I apparently even borrowed James J. Martin's *Men against the State* from the university library: when I read it in 2008, I discovered that the last person to check it out had been my seventeen-year-old self.

But I was certainly primed to reconsider my political beliefs. I was coming to see human lives as richly interconnected, to acknowledge the importance of community in a way that I was unsure how to square with my visceral individualism. At the same time, I was learning more about unjust violence and grinding poverty around the world. I was beginning to view myself as personally responsible for meeting the needs of the world's poor. I was increasingly aware of the arbitrary, unfair, sometimes devastatingly cruel behavior of people in non-state institutions. I was simultaneously learning about the importance of looking critically at the power and position of the wealthy and influential—a critical habit of mind that still seems to me to be of central political importance—and, less valuably, the assumption that statist responses to abuses of power were sensible and, indeed, unavoidable. I breathed in statism, not because anyone with whom I engaged was involved in a malign conspiracy against freedom, but because politically and socially and morally sensitive people, whose critical judgments I shared, simply assumed that state action was the best route to solving the problems they rightly identified.

I didn't see that individualism and concern for genuine community were entirely compatible (we are, as Sheldon Richman rightly says, *molecular* individuals). I didn't realize the importance of asking about the role of state action in creating and maintaining poverty and hierarchy. I supposed uncritically that the right response to poverty and exclusion was state action. And I ignored the capacity of people acting outside the ambit of the state to address these problems.

Still, a generalized awareness of the reality of injustice and oppression and the generally unquestioned assumption that the state was best positioned to deal with unfairness and abuse might not have been enough to make me a full-blown statist. I believe that what really pushed me over the edge, during the latter part of my college experience and at the beginning of my time in graduate school was being grasped by the idea of *negative responsibility*—by the notion that we are as responsible for events that occur as a result of our omissions (whether or not intended) as we are for events that occur as a result of our deliberate acts. Given other things I believed, it seemed as if I were committed also to believing that, when I failed to provide resources to a poor person anywhere in the world, I was responsible for any harm she or he underwent if the money I could have given her would likely have prevented it. Whenever someone died because I hadn't given her or him money, I was, on this view, a murderer.

I was simply overwhelmed at the thought that I was responsible for everyone, for everything, that any time I wanted to spend money on anything I would need to justify doing so in a way that made clear how the expenditure represented a net benefit to the world's poor. And I believe that this way of thinking was what pushed me over the edge

69

into full-blown statism: if the state got involved in redistributing wealth from everyone, the problem could (somehow, I imagined) be put to an end. What I could never do on my own, the state could do. In any event, with a state committed to redistribution, responsibility would be shared, and I wouldn't have to bear an overwhelming burden of guilt.

I believe that being a morally responsible person means being willing to do something about deprivation and economic insecurity. Subordination (whether at the hands of government thugs or courtesy of bosses, parents, teachers, or church leaders) makes life miserable for many people. Exclusion (on such irrational bases as ethnicity, sexual identity or orientation, age, gender, or nationality) stinks. I think I was and am clearly right to oppose all three. It's just unfortunate that I didn't realize that doing so didn't entail supporting the state.

My movement toward statism didn't keep me from defending a radically anarchist political manifesto on the "Wally George Hot Seat," an Orange County TV show hosted by a long-haired Republican media personality. I meant what I said on the show about the evils of the Reagan administration's military adventurism and my opposition to the draft and the death penalty (except for Wally) quite sincerely. But my stint on the "Hot Seat" probably represented the swan song of my college libertarianism.

V

While I finished an undergraduate degree in history and political science, I'd taken a lot of courses in religion and philosophy, and I ultimately decided to focus on philosophical theology and theological ethics in graduate school. I received a PhD in 1991 from the University of Cambridge, in England, after completing a dissertation about the idea of friendship.

The political opinions I embraced as an American graduate student in England were, in general, fairly conventional. While I was skeptical about American bullying and militarism (my views of war probably reflected more of Rothbard's salutary influence than I realized), I was otherwise an unremarkable statist, endorsing what I called a "pragmatic, mixed-economy approach" to economic policy and cheering for European monetary union (motivated by a laudable suspicion of nationalism, I somehow ignored the threats posed by supra-national political institutions).

My dissertation gave me opportunities to think about a variety of moral and political questions. And it certainly prompted some reflection on the limits of, and alternatives to, state authority. I agreed with E. M. Forster that it might well make sense to betray one's country rather than a friend. I argued that a politics sensitive to the reality and value of friendship would involve the devolution of power to small-scale, local institutions in which friendship groups could make a difference (somehow, I couldn't quite make the leap to anarchism). I began to read the work of philosopher Stephen R. L. Clark, whose *Civil Peace and Sacred Order* demolished conventional rationales for the legitimacy of state power. I have often thought in retrospect that Stephen's sensible arguments cured me of any sort of theoretical statism, though I can remember no crisis of statist conscience occasioned by any of this. And my reading and personal experience brought home to me my fondness for the New Left's vision of a decentralized, participatory society. It's easy to see a convergence between a call for radical decentralization designed to make friendship as politically meaningful as it was in the ancient Greek *polis* and a call for decentralization rooted in the conviction that rule by large-scale, impersonal bureaucracies is alienating and dehumanizing. But I didn't draw systematically anti-statist conclusions.

VI

I defended my dissertation in September of 1991. Back in California, I clocked a couple of volunteer hours for Bill Clinton's presidential campaign, even though I'd found him untrustworthy during the primary season. After the November election, I relished the arrival of a new administration that would, I was sure, improve things significantly for workers and poor people. And in January of 1993, I found a new reason to think about politics: I was hired as the editor of a weekly newspaper.

As a newspaper editor, I learned about the use of sales-tax and other incentives to attract Wal-Mart stores to municipalities. I angrily criticized a local state legislator's plan to "fatten the turkeys" by declining to execute juveniles convicted of putatively capital crimes while killing them once they'd reached the age of majority. Drawn, regrettably, to cultural conservatism, I defended public schools as necessary for the transmission of common values and stories. And I reflected on what seemed to me to be the sex-negativity embodied in some then-current discussions of sexual harassment. But I didn't experience any blinding insights, and I didn't question the statism I blithely assumed.

During the same period, I spent time thinking about the value of workplace democracy as an antidote to bosses' tyranny. Increasingly convinced that work-lives structured by employment relationships were pretty awful, I came to realize that unions could be vital contributors to the process of moving toward more humane work environments, though with the long-term goal clearly being full-blown worker self-management.

I declined to vote a second time for Clinton when he signed the 1996 welfare reform bill, opting for Ralph Nader instead. But I was initially oblivious to Clinton's imperialistic misadventures (as in the Balkans) and to the domestic authoritarianism reflected in the militia scare and the Antiterrorism and Effective Death Penalty Act (though I certainly remembered his calculated approval of Arkansas's execution of mentally disabled Ricky Ray Rector during the 1992 campaign).

During this period, I continued to return periodically to the issues related to personal wealth that had helped to push me over the edge toward statism. I certainly didn't want to be overwhelmed with responsibility for the world. But I also didn't want to lapse into a moral somnambulism, ignoring the real needs of hurting people in the real world. I needed a clearer sense of what was morally reasonable. As I spent more time thinking about moral philosophy, I was increasingly drawn toward the "new classical natural law" theory. A contemporary development of Aquinas's natural position, it provided a clear explanation of the in-principle impossibility of consequentialisms of all kinds and of the wrongness of capital punishment and aggressive war. It tracked my moral instincts well, exhibited considerable illuminating power, and, most importantly for me on a visceral level, simultaneously showed why I had real responsibilities for those other than myself while denying validity to the calls for unlimited responsibility that continued to terrify me.

VII

I spent most of the '90s frustrated because the academic jobs I wanted eluded me. In the fall of 1998, I finally decided to enroll in law school at UCLA, hoping a law degree would open up another path toward academic employment.

In law school, of course, everything one did had political dimensions. But I had no real occasion for reflecting critically on my statism. I was even, disturbingly, willing to consider some state restrictions on free speech legitimate. Certainly, as I wrote papers, I took the authority of the state for granted.

In retrospect, I find this odd: I certainly knew that standard defenses of state authority were unsuccessful. Perhaps it was just that I identified reflexively with members of the political class, assumed that what I was doing was designed to guide them, and simply treated the institutions they oversaw as givens because I had instinctively adopted their point of view and wanted to be one of them. I'm still not sure; I'm quite sure I didn't really believe state authority was rooted in the consent of the governed—after all, Stephen Clark had long since shown me otherwise.

VIII

After law school, I joined the full-time faculty of the La Sierra University School of Business.

My work at the School of Business might have been thought to prompt me to rethink my statism—encouraging me to take markets more seriously because my colleagues were market-friendly—but it's not obvious that it did. And perhaps that's not surprising: most of the students and colleagues with whom I interacted in this period were hardly hardy market enthusiasts. With some honorable exceptions, most business people, after all, are quite happy for the state to protect their property values with zoning regulations and protect their business positions with tariffs, cartels, patents, and licensing and other regulations.

In any case, the articles I wrote during my first few years as a business faculty member continued to assume the legitimacy of state power. For instance: while, in a piece about tax policy, I offered some arguments against the existence of an entity like the Internal Revenue Service, with the ability to review individual financial records and seize personal assets, the notion that no taxing authority at all might be legitimate doesn't seem to have crossed my mind. In general, I was still uncritically inclined to make the unjustified leap from "There is good reason to want such-and-such an institution or social practice to be in place" to "The state can and should bring the institution or practice in question into being."

My spirit was still clearly libertarian, though—more than I realized at the time. I can tell because, despite my self-identification as a socialist, more than one decidedly un-libertarian friend tweaked me intermittently regarding my opposition to institutional authoritarianism using the dreaded l-word: "Well, for a libertarian like you . . . ."

IX

While my time in the School of Business didn't, at least at first, do much to turn me against the state, events on the national political scene did.

In the course of a few months after September 11, 2001, George W. Bush went from being a forgettable mediocrity to being, along with Woodrow Wilson, one of the two most authoritarian presidents elected in the twentieth century. He invaded Afghanistan, forced through the USA PATRIOT Act, and attacked Iraq.

The high-handedness, the lawlessness, the evident disregard for just war norms reflected in the move toward the attack on Iraq infuriated me beyond words. I was scheduled to preach a sermon less than a week after the attack began. One of my assigned texts was the

Ten Commandments; I angrily explained how the Bush Administration had violated, was violating, all ten.

No one in the White House or the Pentagon seemed to care.

Bush arrested people, held them without trial, and claimed legalistically that constitutional norms didn't apply because they weren't American citizens, or hadn't been seized in the United States. And then we found out about the Bush-authorized domestic surveillance program. And the Abu-Ghraib atrocities. And the systematic torture of political prisoners.

The Bush Administration's track record of abuse served as a salutary reminder of just how much harm can be done when the state has power. It made me considerably more suspicious of the state.

My suspicion only grew when the Democrats retook both houses of Congress, and proceeded—with the support of Barack Obama—to do exactly nothing about the Bush Administration's abuses. It turned to disgust when the Obama Administration roared into office. Obama appointed a paid-up member of the War Party as his Secretary of State. He rushed to defend Bush-era policies regarding state secrets. He authorized cosmetic changes that seemed likely to underwrite the continued use of torture (and would, of course, go on to embrace legislation permitting indefinite detention without trial). He endorsed efforts designed superficially to reduce the US government's presence in Iraq while stepping up its military activities in Afghanistan. On the domestic front, he made clear that he was happy to continue a chummy relationship with the corporatocracy, cheerily continuing corporate bailouts that principled people on both sides of the aisle had opposed. In short, he seemed happy to be serving George W. Bush's third term.

X

The political and military malfeasance I saw just tended to confirm the rightness of the libertarian—now anarchist—position to which I was increasingly returning.

I had begun to think about anarchy and the philosophy of law during Bush's second term, though I cannot now identify just what prompted my return to anarchist texts and issues. Perhaps I had recently reread some of Stephen Clark's pointed discussions of anarchism. In any event, in the fall of 2005, I began writing an article called "Disaggregating Legal Obligation" that argued, in effect, that binding legal obligations flowed from independent moral requirements, and that purely positive legal injunctions were unlikely to be authoritative. By 2008, frustrated by the growth of the warfare state, I was investigating non-state alternatives to military defense. I found myself reading scholarly articles about law and anarchy and then, without warning, discovered that I was hard at work defending anarchism in an article subsequently accepted for publication in the *Oxford Journal of Legal Studies*.

I certainly didn't see myself as having abandoned the Left—just the *statist* Left. But I *was* invested in the anarchist project. But I wouldn't have been entirely comfortable re-identifying as a libertarian. The label seemed to me associated, somehow, with lack of concern for consumers and the poor—I still found it hard to imagine that economically vulnerable people didn't need the state—and valorization of business titans.

What really made the difference was my discovery of Kevin Carson's work. Carson's brilliance floored me (as did the fact that he found time and energy to produce massive theoretical works while working full-time, not as a professor or journalist, but as a hospital orderly; he was certainly no business titan). He had successfully integrated a set of striking insights, showing that

- small-scale organizational structures—more humane, more just, more livable—turn out to be more economically efficient, and so likely to emerge in a liberated—*freed*—market absent state support for hierarchical behemoths;

- past violence and continuing statist privilege, rather than private ownership, are responsible for wealth concentration and the ability of the owners of capital to push people around;

- given that the property of many large corporations is really theirs only because of state action, this property need not be

76

treated as owned legitimately by them and would thus be ripe for homesteading even in a free-market legal order in which legitimate property rights are treated as inviolable, so that the redistribution of this property is justified precisely on free market grounds (an insight I could, of course, have gleaned decades earlier from Rothbard).

Echoing Rothbard, Carson helped me to acknowledge the importance of a genuinely libertarian theory of class, one that didn't pretend that there weren't social classes, but which instead acknowledged forthrightly that there were, while emphasizing that it was someone's relationship with the state that determined her class position. Unprincipled people with wealth can influence the political process in ways that solidifies their wealth and power and guarantees that they will have access to privileges that keep them wealthy and powerful. And people who gain political power, whatever their initial motives, can and do use it to exploit ordinary people while becoming members of the elite themselves. In both ways, then, the state helps to ensure the existence and power of a privileged class.

Before engaging with Carson's work, I had shared the instinctual view of many people on the Left that talk about markets was a smoke-screen for corporate power-grabs. He made clear why it often was precisely this, but why markets distorted by privilege were nothing at all like genuinely freed markets. He showed me a way to link the various kinds of anti-authoritarianism that all seemed to matter to me emotionally. I could oppose state power and corporate power at the same time. I could combine the desire for real freedom that had motivated my libertarianism with the commitment to opposing exclusion, deprivation, and subordination (along with aggressive and preventive war) that I embraced as a leftist.

I knew that, on a deep, visceral level, I resonated with libertarians like Carson on issues related to war and empire; immigration freedom; opposition to tariffs, intellectual "property," occupational licensure, land use rules, and the regulation of sex, drugs, and gambling; the value of replacing criminal law with tort law; and civil liberties. I could see why a system that allowed for the application of tort law on a case-by-case basis by juries could achieve the desirable goals of state regulation with lower costs and greater flexibility. I agreed that the state consistently made and kept people poor (sometimes by horrible accident, sometimes in the course of securing privileges for the wealthy and well connected). I resonated with arguments for the view that, without state props for the wealthy and well connected, work-life would improve, that many more people would work for themselves or as participants in partnerships or cooperatives, and that, where employment for wages persisted, unions—fully voluntary, and disentangled from the state—would be able to win meaningful victories for workers, who would enjoy much stronger bargaining positions than they do in an environment distorted by statist privilege.

XI

I also realized that the state need not be seen as necessary to protect the poor. Eliminating a variety of state privileges would ensure, I realized, that far fewer people suffered from poverty. And people could reasonably be expected to organize social services effectively and efficiently in the state's absence.

Thus, for instance: the current debate about health care focused on folding currently uninsured people into the existing, high-priced health-care system while funneling money to well-connected insurers. But I realized that, if the goal was to increase access to health care, that goal could be achieved by

- ending state policies that make and keep people poor;

- eliminating policies that raise the cost of living;

- ending policies that increase the cost of health-care in particular, including professional licensing requirements, hospital accreditation requirements, drug patents, medical device patents, limitations on competition among insurance agencies, and tax preferences for employer-purchased health insurance; and

- pursuing structural changes that will increase overall levels of wealth and discretionary income.

Various things could cause economic vulnerability and insecurity even in a genuinely freed market. What I realized, however, was that it was fallacious to suppose that *the state* was needed to address these problems.

XII

Radical libertarians like Carson, Roderick Long, Sheldon Richman, Brad Spangler, Tom Knapp, Charles W. Johnson, and Joe Stromberg, I realized, didn't like to see people pushed around. Neither did I. They weren't corporate shills. They weren't pot-smoking Republicans. They were leftists. They were my kind of people.

Through their work, I was redirected to the work of the prototypical American anarchist Benjamin Tucker, to whom Rothbard had first exposed me in the early '80s. I realized that Tucker had pointed the way toward the realization that a commitment to *socialism* was thoroughly compatible with unequivocal support for *markets* entirely freed from state-secured privilege.

Eliminating privileges—tariffs, patents, copyrights, limits on banking freedom, land engrossment, subsidies, licenses, cartels, etc.—would address the problems of poverty and worker disempowerment, along with the vast wealth disparities that conferred great influence on some and marginalized others. These problems—the "social question" with which the earliest socialists, like Tucker, were concerned—could be resolved precisely by eliminating the monopolistic privileges of the wealthy and well connected.

The power of capitalists was dependent on the power of the state; thus, over time, a genuinely freed market could be expected to lead to a wide dispersion of wealth and a dramatic reduction in social and organizational hierarchy. Thus, socialism need not be *state* socialism, it need not involve anything like mandatory collective ownership, and it was perfectly compatible with freed markets. Socialist goals could be achieved using market means.

That was exciting. So was rediscovering an aspect of my past. I'd been a natural fit for the libertarian movement in a lot of ways, but I'd left it behind because I had mistakenly believed that being a libertarian meant being a rightist. Now, I was able to reenter the libertarian world.

I am very pleased to have found a way to integrate my formative political passion for freedom—my visceral distaste for being, or seeing others be, pushed around—with my deep-seated moral opposition to exclusion, deprivation, and subordination. I've discovered how to be both a committed leftist and a committed libertarian.

What would Amandine think? Full-fledged libertarian at fifteen. Full-fledged socialist at twenty-one. By forty-two—both.

End Notes

1.   Though they were harder to classify than the labels might suggest. Unlike many other self-described conservative Republicans, they strongly favored church-state separation and abortion rights. And my dad decried the Catholic minority's feudalistic economic dominance in Vietnam.

Dorothy Colegrove
Chemist; Bitterroot Valley, MT

Dorothy Colegrove was born and raised in the Atlanta, GA metropolitan area. She attended Kennesaw State University and completed her BS in chemistry in 2003. After attempting one year of graduate school in Indiana, she decided she would rather enter the workforce instead of pursuing a PhD. She lived in Florida, Georgia, Massachusetts, New Hampshire, and Washington and now resides with her husband in the Bitterroot Valley area of southwestern Montana. She worked in a number of industries as a chemist, and currently commutes to work every two weeks in Prudhoe Bay, Alaska. Always a Georgian native at heart, but not always a Georgia resident, Dorothy hopes to see taxation changes (Go Fair Tax!) before returning to a state with both sales and personal income taxes. When not working, she has her nose buried in an old-fashioned printed book. Refugee memoirs are a personal favorite, with contemporary romance a close second. One day she hopes to compete on "Jeopardy!", but first she has to wade through her least favorite literary genres: classic American and English literature.

Chemist Discovers the Libertarian Recipe
by
Dorothy Colegrove

My strongest personality trait is that I will stand up and speak for others when they are unable or unwilling to stand up and speak for themselves. These emotions become strongest when my core sense of right and wrong is violated. The United States Declaration of Independence lists unalienable (i.e. inalienable) rights based upon the idea of natural rights established by God and nature. When another person or entity threatens inalienable rights, I feel a compulsion to stand up and speak out against the threat.

The behavior of my family members created my moral foundation. As a child growing up in the suburbs of Atlanta, my father taught me that racism was inexcusable and being a helpful citizen to others was a necessary behavior. He is the kind of man that starts conversations with strangers. He will help the stranded motorist move their vehicle from traffic. His repeated acts of kindness when I was a child created a great role model. I declared myself a Democrat and especially a liberal because the Left wants to take care of people and make them better. The Left would save the world via the government. I thought this was the best way to emulate the behavior of standing up for others and helping them in their times of need. After 19.5 years, I discovered I was wrong.

Memory tells me that my parents were apolitical in the 1980s and early '90s. I remember vague references to politics during presidential campaign years, but nothing detailed. My only memory concerning politics was watching the evening news in 1984 and seeing Walter Mondale.

Unlike my parents, my maternal relatives are all staunch Republicans. From age five, my maternal grandparents would discuss politics, current events, and history with me. My maternal grandfather was a West Point graduate and Korean War veteran. He and my grandmother were small business owners for more than 40 years. The political issue I remember my grandparents discussing the most was taxes. As small business owners and investors, many economic policies affected their ability to invest capital. However, I do not recall any discussion of social political issues. My grandfather would watch CNN's "Crossfire" every evening. He kept the TV on CNN or "Headline News" and later "Fox News." I did not watch cartoons with him. However, even with my exposure to news propaganda, I learned my political ideology in the public school system. I shunned my maternal uncles and grandparents Republican label.

Although I grew up with staunch Republican family members, I was a very vocal liberal in high school. In political science essays, I wrote enthusiastically of the *rightness* of socialism. I really believed that the high taxation typical of Scandinavian countries was the ideal form of government. I remember having a debate with my three uncles when I was 17 about how *right* I was and how *wrong* they were. Yes, the government should pay for maternity leave. Yes, welfare should support anyone. High taxes were the population's payment for living in a healthy, free society.

I took a pre-college course in politics at Brown University in Providence, RI and read President Clinton's Secretary of Labor, Robert Reich's, book *Locked in the Cabinet*. I was such an elitist snob that I did *not* read the Thomas Sowell book assigned for the class (*The Vision of the Anointed*) and only partially read the Newt Gingrich title, *To Renew America*. I was the typical know-it-all teenager.

My email address was "liberalchick"—that is how much my political identity was my actual identity. Originally, I planned to go to George Washington University in Washington DC, to major in international affairs. I changed my mind about the school after seeing a video that made it look like a party school. I declined their offer and went to Smith College in Massachusetts.

Any good female liberal should be familiar with Smith. While Smith has Barbara Bush and Nancy Reagan among its alumnae, the feminists Betty Friedan and Gloria Steinem are the women I wanted to emulate. However, I only lasted a semester there. At the time, I thought it was because Smith did not take my 35 college credits I had completed while in high school—looking back, I realize that I was subconsciously rebelling against the hyper-liberal atmosphere.

I left Smith and returned to Georgia. I continued liberal self-identification for another year—until February 2000. This was the month I completed my taxes for my first full year living on my own. After leaving Smith, I used capital gains proceeds to pay for my housing while I attended Kennesaw State University in Kennesaw, GA. I had my own apartment and all the expenses that come with being a 19-year-old who does not understand "estimated taxes" and how to calculate capital gains using 1999 tax tables. I quickly learned that stock shares gifted to me in the 1980s prior to the stock market boom of the 90s had split and triple-split multiple times and were essentially 100% taxable. I was looking at a tax bill of nearly $20,000.

My great-grandmother gave me stock to provide for school so I did not have to work or take out student loans. I felt like, "What the hell? I am paying someone's welfare check! This is BS!" Here I was, yes, a somewhat financially irresponsible 19-year-old, but I did not drink alcohol, nor do drugs. I just went to school full-time, pursuing a degree in chemistry. Now the government demanded $20,000 from me. It made me stop and investigate the "loopholes" for the rich. Turns out, the idea of loopholes was just a liberal delusion. My family members informed me, "No, you have to pay. No, we don't get around it." I started to realize that maybe this was not in line with my politics. Why should I pay for someone else's poor decisions?

I always identified with liberalism because of the "leave my body alone" politics of pro-choice, pro-drug legalization, pro-prostitution and could not identify with Republicans because of the lack of body freedom. An Atlanta-based talk radio host, Neal Boortz, introduced me to libertarianism. I researched the party and realized that I was a fiscal conservative and social liberal. Government should not be a source of charity. The people should be the source. Where was the motivation to stay in school and make smart decisions in the liberal model of government? Higher taxes punish financially successful people that made responsible decisions.

The nail in the coffin of liberalism came in 2005 with my grandfather's death. I already self-identified as a libertarian, but I will *never* change my mind after what happened with his death. My great-grandmother passed away in 1998. She had a 10-year charitable trust. One of her three heirs, my grandmother, died within that 10-year period. My grandmother's heir was my grandfather. He also died in that 10-year period. The nastiness of death taxes hit the *same* money *three times*. Neither heir had ever possessed the money while alive. The money did not have a chance to earn interest. It made me disgusted. According to one of my socialist acquaintances, the intent of death taxes is to "prevent the formation of aristocracy," but that kind of taxation is punitive. What is the point of working hard for yourself and your heirs if the government punishes you at death?

I realized in my conversion to libertarianism, that it is possible to be a helpful, kind, and charitable citizen without being a liberal. In my opinion, too many liberals ignore private charities by operating under the delusion that government redistribution of tax dollars is the better solution. I feel more personal satisfaction from my individual acts than I feel when I look at my paycheck and see the withheld payroll taxes. I can emulate the behavior I saw from my father. I have been told I am "not like other white people" when it comes to my views on racism, prejudice, and discrimination. I do not have to be a Democrat to care about the success and prosperity of minorities. That statement may sound trivial to someone that does not have strong feelings on those issues, but for me, I passionately believe that God created all people equal. Government lacks the divine right to take away a person's life, liberty, or property.

Eleven years after my conversion, I work in one of the most politicized locations in the United States. I work in the field of project management in the Prudhoe Bay oilfield in Alaska. I spend at least two weeks of every four away from my family in order to provide financial support. I make the sacrifice of living without them for more than half the year. Many people tell me, "How can you handle it? I just couldn't do it. I couldn't be away from my family. It's so cold up there! Don't you feel lonely?"

I do not understand why anyone has these qualms. If you need to support your family financially, you should be willing to make sacrifices. My taxes are higher because of all the overtime I accumulate working 12 hour days for two weeks at a time. I am disgusted every paycheck by the high percentage that is stolen from me because I am willing to sacrifice my time with my family by working away from them. Every paycheck reinforces my politics by the ever-growing amount of federal and state taxes. However, I do not let my outrage with the government impede my behavior with individuals. I will help the lost stranger in the airport that does not speak English and cannot find her way. I will donate money, items, and time to private charities. I will send books overseas to help educate a friend's children. I can be a libertarian and be a good person, regardless of what some liberals may feel. Libertarians are not narcissists. We care about our fellow human beings enough to want them to be free to make their own choices and control their destinies.

Michael W. Dean
Writer and Film Director; Casper, WY

Michael W. Dean writes non-fiction books and directs documentary films. His works include *$30 Film School*, *D.I.Y. or Die: How to Survive as an Independent Artist*, and *Guns and Weed: The Road to Freedom*. He has toured Europe and America speaking at colleges, museums, and youth centers. Michael sang in the punk bands The Beef People, Baby Opaque, Bomb, and Right Arm of Wyoming. He enjoys his wife, guns, cats, and liberty. Don't tread on him.

Movie: www.gunsandweed.com

Podcast: www.freedomfeens.com

Blog: www.libertarianpunk.com

Buy a Gun, Lose All Your Friends
by
Michael W. Dean

I lived in San Francisco and Los Angeles for 26 of my 47 years. I was attracted to the laissez-faire attitude toward sex, drugs, and rock 'n' roll. I'd always been a bit rebellious against authority, getting kicked out of two schools as a kid for "attitude problems" despite scoring above the 90th percentile in everything. I felt I was too smart for school, and maybe I was right.

I moved to California at age 19. Left a small town in upstate New York that I felt was too "square" to inspire or contain me.

I always voted Democrat, but wasn't very active in politics. I never knew what my politics were, but I knew what they *weren't*. I didn't want to be a stuffy old selfish Republican, so I knew that I had to be the "opposite" of a Republican. I figured I was a Democrat, since I was compassionate and not square. It never really occurred to me when I was young that the "compassion" of Democrats (and Republicans) comes from stealing money from people to give to others. And that this stealing occurs *literally* at gunpoint. (If you don't pay your taxes, they'll send men with guns to your home to arrest you, and if you resist, they'll point those guns at your head, and possibly shoot you.) It never occurred to me that that isn't really "charity."

I used to vote Democrat. But I couldn't really tell you why. I hated authority and I hated big government. I guess I just wasn't paying attention. I was one of those folks who thought that following the issues was too much work. So I voted by clipping out the little voting guide from the leftie *City Paper.* (A chain that has papers in most major cities. It's so left as to be practically communist, and as Jim Goad said "it's free and worth every penny.") Voting the way the paper told me is how, decades ago, I ended up voting for Dianne Feinstein and Nancy Pelosi. I consider a lot of what I do now to be making amends to society for that.

The first time I encountered libertarians was in the student union at my college. They had a card table set up and were trying to appeal to passers-by with the marijuana legalization angle. Even though I smoked pot at the time, I avoided those people. They seemed like they were on a *mission. . . .*they were almost *religious*, and that scared me off.

Later, in San Francisco, I considered myself and all my friends hip because we thought we rejected authority. But hypocritically, we voted for people who wanted to impose much more authority in almost every measure of our lives. Hell, you can't even buy a Big Mac in San Francisco anymore, and they're trying to outlaw *pet stores*. California politics have been described as "a cross between Mother Theresa and Stalin." (One-time San Francisco mayor Art Agnos coined that term, not as a pejorative, but as something he was looking for in people to implement his plans!)

Somewhere along the line I heard that quote attributed to Churchill, "If you're not a liberal at twenty you have no heart, if you're not a conservative at forty you have no brain." I said to myself "I'll *never* be conservative." I was right, in the "George W. Bush Christian Sharia conservative" sense, but I did later change my registration to Republican for about a year.

Everyone I knew in California considered themselves to be full of acceptance. But they were entirely unaccepting of anyone who would *dare* vote Republican. You could probably be a child molester and be more accepted by many Californians than be a Republican, and that's barely hyperbole.

They say the thing that keeps you from getting old is your ability to learn and change. My politics didn't change until I was 40. And the stepping stone was, of all things, guns, which I'd always been afraid of

I'm a peace lovin' guy. I'd never hurt anyone who did not try to hurt me. But I love guns. I've got one on me right now. I have two more a few feet away, and they're all loaded. To me guns are symbols of, and protectors of, liberty. Libertarianism is based on the idea of "do not initiate aggression." But if you have no way to *stop* aggression, I believe you aren't a very effective libertarian.

Four years ago I was awake late one night in my home in Los Angeles when someone outside tried to pry open our bedroom window. The guy wasn't very badass. Unarmed, I chased him away just by going outside and confronting him.

But my wife and I were shaken. The next day I told Debra, "Baby, we're buying a shotgun." She was very against it. She said, "Buying a gun is admitting that the world is a horrible place." I said, "Baby, sometimes the world *is* a horrible place, and I love you, and I want to protect us."

And being the one California Democrat with his balls intact, I bought a shotgun anyway, even though my wife hated the idea.

Turns out, we both really liked guns, and we loved our dates to the range. We soon added his 'n' hers 9mm pistols and a couple .22 rifles to our collection. Debra became a good shot in weeks. Took me a little longer.

All of our friends were lefties, and most of them were concerned about the "new us." But they still kept talking to us, and we even took one of them to the range. Once.

I started reading up on California and Federal gun laws. I've never been arrested and intended to keep it that way. Debra (a paralegal) and I decided that the laws seemed designed not to protect people from violence, but rather were structured to make honest folks into criminals.

Our new view of nanny-state gun laws made us look at California (and the USA) in a whole new way. And that made us both start paying attention to government and politics. We realized that "politicians steal all your rights and give a tiny bit back in exchange for your vote" and "all elections are advance auctions of stolen goods."

We became libertarians almost overnight.

I got there from "punk rock anarchist" on one end and apolitical liberal Democrat on the other. I loved the process, but it was so fast that it kinda hurt. Debra didn't have as far to go. ... Turns out she was registered Republican and leaned libertarian (and loves the works of Ayn Rand). If I'd known years earlier that she was registered Republican, I probably wouldn't have married her. But it never really came up.

My wife really liked my political "spiritual transformation." Her dad, by the way, had given her Heinlein books to read as a child, and he'd stumped door to door for Goldwater, whom many consider the spiritual godfather of the Libertarian Party.

Debra and I got itchy. Being around leftists suddenly gave us hives. So it was clear what we had to do: GET OUT OF CALIFORNIA AND MOVE TO WYOMING. We did our research, and liked Wyoming for its beauty, its low population, its lack of punitive gun laws, its good economy, low population and lack of state income tax.

Our leftist friends got even more worried. One said, "OK, I guess I can 'get' having a shotgun for protection, if you must. But I really don't feel comfortable coming to a house with handguns in it, and. . . . WAIT. . . . YOU DON'T HAVE THEM WITH YOU NOW, in MY house, do you?!!"

Or, "Who is this 'Ron Paul person you say you're voting for? Libertarian? What's a 'libertarian'?" And "Obama is so cool and hip and . . . wait, WHAT? YOU'RE SELLING YOUR HOUSE AND MOVING TO WYOMING? And you wanna buy a BATTLE RIFLE? What the hell is a BATTLE RIFLE?!"

I now have a lot more to talk about with my dad and my father-in-law. I no longer think they're "square", and I really love yakking with them now. They "get it."

We love that our new friends and neighbors are far less "in other people's business" than most everyone we met in California. Which is partly because our new friends and neighbors are nicer people, and partly because most of them own and carry guns, too. (As Robert Heinlein noted, "An armed society is a polite society.")

We've lived in Wyoming for two years and WE LOVE IT. The air is clean, the people are sweet, the economy is stable, and we can carry a pistol, or have our loaded battle rifle on the car seat next to us. Talk about "breathing in the sweet air of liberty!"

Carrying a gun could literally get you killed by SWAT in California. Here, people just say, "Oh, my husband has that one! Is that the .357 or the .44?" or "Nice rifle! Getting in shape for antelope season?"

Our few remaining leftie friends back in California who still talked to us followed this ongoing transformation in words and pictures on my blog. One by one they STOPPED BEING OUR FRIENDS. Their comments ranged from a good friend of eight years saying "Michael, I love you, but I'm really worried about you" to a good friend of 23 years (a guy I was in a band with) saying, "Michael. . . . Once someone gets talked into these right-wing ideas very rarely can they be talked back. . . . This new-found cocky way of life is very wrong, very immoral and very dangerous. I'm older than you so consider my opinion, if you still can. . . . I doubt you will. This makes me very sad. Good luck, dumb fuck."

Another "friend" actually talked about *organizing an intervention* and driving out here to "save us." Didn't happen though. I guess it's easier to take the bottle out of a passed-out drunk's hand than it is to take guns away from people who are more awake and alive than they've ever been.

Even strangers chimed in. Typical of the many slams I received was a fan of my older books and music who said "I can't believe how quickly you went from being a cool, artistic guy to being a WalMart redneck Red Lobster-eating gun-toting asshole."

The comments from strangers made me laugh, in a dropped-jaw kind of way. The comments from the actual friends hurt a little. But I remembered what my dear sweet mother would have said: "If they say things like that, they're not really your friends." And my always dad told me, "Better to find out now than further down the road."

I do not cling to my "victimhood" and you'll never catch me at a support group or on Oprah bitching about this (nor would she have me). All in all it has really just reinforced my resolve to reject idiocy in all its forms.

I just cannot wrap my head around the fact that so many people, including ones I thought were "cool", cannot wrap THEIR heads around the fact that "social justice" is always accomplished by muggery and thuggery. And they get freaked out if I say "Guns aren't bad, guns are good. . . . And guns make it harder to be a victim of muggery and thuggery."

I changed my registration from Democrat to Republican and got involved in Wyoming politics. There are a few libertarian Republicans in the state government here, and I was trying to bring more in. I gave up when I finally realized that even though Wyoming Republicans generally want to "let" you carry a concealed weapon without a permit, many still consider it their *moral duty* to throw people in cages for all sorts of non-violent things, from gambling to smoking a joint if you're dying of cancer.

I'm no longer involved with the Republican Party (or any party). I'm into ALL rights, not just "single-issue rights", and I think I can accomplish that better through education than through politics. I think the whole system is a sham. Even if you ARE into the system, "lesser of two evil" voting will always get you *some* evil.

I consider myself libertarian, which, to me, is more an all-encompassing philosophical designation than just a political idea. The word "libertarian" means "the opposite of authoritarian." Libertarians are into freedom and personal liberty, and do not like authoritarians imposing restrictions on them.

Those other folks can just stay in California while it fiscally crashes and drops into the economic sea. My wife and I will be in Wyoming. If you need us, we're probably on a date to the rifle range. After that we'll be at Red Lobster, then WalMart.

Jennifer Eklund
Homeschooling mother and doctoral student in psychology; Carmichael, CA

Jennifer Eklund is a homeschooling mother of two beautiful, intelligent children. She lives in Carmichael, CA with her children, boyfriend, a dog, and a cat. She enjoys reading non-fiction, playing poker, and writing. Jennifer spent every Saturday night throughout the racing season at the All American Speedway in Roseville, CA which turned her into a lifelong NASCAR fan. She's known as the family stalker due to her passion for genealogy, something she inherited from her paternal grandmother.

She earned a Bachelor of Science in psychology from the University of Phoenix in 2009. She went on to earn a Master of Science in psychology with a specialization in social psychology from Walden University in 2011. She is currently studying for a doctorate degree in psychology with a specialization in gender diversity at North Central University. Jennifer is a strong supporter of online education. It affords access to education for individuals who might not have the ability to otherwise achieve their educational goals. Jennifer works at home writing genealogy curriculum and scoring achievement tests for two national scoring companies. Jennifer would like to write non-fiction, teach psychology courses online, and continue to advocate for equal rights. She is currently developing a non-profit home school organization called Rainbow Homeschoolers that will provide home school support for all family types.

Evolving Toward the Party of Freedom
by
Jennifer Eklund

Growing up, I constantly heard the phrase, "Clear your plate. There are starving children in Ethiopia." I watched the "We are the World" video over and over, which brought attention to famine in Africa. Meanwhile, Ronald Reagan was president in the 1980s through the bulk of my childhood. During the Reagan era, America was seen as the world's superpower. Add these variables to the mind of a little girl living in a dual-earner middle-class family and I could not for the life of me figure out why America had starving children, homeless people, orphaned children, or why America had not solved the world's problems. Was that not our job as the world's superpower?

In 6th grade, a class project required us to choose a political party. Republican or Democrat, there was no other choice. My juvenile understanding of these two political parties was that Republicans were greedy capitalists who wanted to take away the right for a woman to have an abortion and Democrats were the saviors who were trying to help those in need and continue the right for a woman to choose. This was before I learned about stereotypes and the dangers of grouping individuals into all or nothing categories. I chose to be a Democrat for the project. At 18 years old, I registered as a Democrat. In my first election, 1996, I voted for Bill Clinton for president, helping in my own little way to secure his second term.

I married into a Republican family. My father-in-law would constantly tell me that by 30 I would be a Republican. I would roll my eyes and think he was nuts. No way would I ever support a party that was more about money and their mansions, than taking care of Americans. I was in my early 20s and still had not learned about the dangers of stereotypes. I supported an America that forced the rich to take care of the less fortunate. If people wouldn't make moral decisions to help feed and clothe the poor, then the government had every right to do so. The Democratic Party was the only party that believed in true freedom and equality toward the American dream.

Anyone who was not a Democrat was a mean individual who did not care about human beings.

Throughout my 20s I started to learn what being a Democrat really meant. I began to view the party without my rose-colored glasses. Their policies seemed to keep the poor, poor. Their policies were not about freedom. My attitude and beliefs started to change when I had children. I saw that the Republican Party was not a group of evil capitalists bent on seeing Americans die daily from starvation and the conditions of homelessness. I started to believe that every American has the right to make money and spend their money the way they choose. This belief appeared when I realized that taxes for social programs impeded my ability to provide everything I wanted for my children.

Another startling revelation occurred when Governor Gray Davis was forced into a recall election in 2003 with Republican actor Arnold Schwarzenegger. I was determined to see Governor Davis continue on as California's governor. I was eager to vote for him and found the reasons for the recall election to be preposterous. A couple of weeks before the election, Governor Davis stated that if re-elected, he would ensure that illegal immigrants be granted driver's licenses and make illegal immigrants eligible for in-state tuition rates at California's public colleges. Why would individuals breaking our laws be allowed a driver's license or be eligible for in-state tuition rates at California's public colleges? When I attended community college in the late 1990s I had a friend from Sweden who attended the college. Her tuition was astronomical. She was here legally, pursuing an education. She was not breaking our laws and if she had broken a law she would have been sent back to Sweden. I realized that Davis being re-elected would not be good for California or America.

The closer 30 came, the more I saw myself becoming a Republican. I was scared. Though I had started to agree with the Republican Party's economic policies for America, their positions on social issues would never jive with my own. Though I had two children and could not imagine having an abortion, I would never take away a woman's right to choose for herself. I'd stay a Democrat and vote for candidates regardless of party. I don't remember ever voting for someone just because they were a Democrat. I always researched the candidates and voted for the candidate that most closely matched my beliefs, whether a Democrat or a Republican. I never looked beyond the two parties for a better candidate. I thought that to do so would be wasting my vote. However, I felt more and more as though the party with which I registered defined me. The more I learned about the Democrat and Republican Parties the more I did not want either label to define me. My mindset was stuck with most of America in the two-party system, so I had to either be a Democrat or a Republican.

In 2008, events in California shocked me into looking for a new party. Proposition 8 was on the ballot. This proposition's purpose was to ban gay marriage in California—keeping marriage between a man and a woman. I was convinced this proposition had no chance in passing. California, one of the most liberal states, would never ban gay marriage. Sexual orientation was not something for which Californian's discriminated against people for.

Despite my confidence in my fellow Californians, Proposition 8 passed and I was left with anger I never before felt concerning politics. I could not understand why two people who love one another could not marry one another and how did a state that voted for Barack Obama for president could deny a group of citizens their Constitutional rights? For months, I processed this inexcusable injustice. I could no longer be a member of a party that sent my conscience into anxious fits. Throughout the 2008 elections, I began to question the ability of the two-party system, and researched all of the candidates to choose the one that best matched my political ideologies. I voted for the Libertarian presidential candidate Bob Barr in the 2008 election because he was not against gay marriage, while Obama and John McCain were. I also agreed with Barr's stance on other issues as well, more than I agreed with Obama and McCain. I started researching the Libertarian Party and considered registering as a Libertarian.

For months, I reflected upon who I was, on my beliefs, and attitudes. Voting Libertarian would take me out of the process, wouldn't it? My vote would never really count because the Libertarian

Party doesn't have the resources or receives the same media attention as the Republicans and Democrats, right? But I wanted to be able to look in the mirror every morning and live in peace with the votes I cast. I wanted to vote for candidates who believe in freedom for everyone, regardless of their personal beliefs about economic and social issues. I wanted to vote for candidates who did not interpret and twist the Constitution for their own benefit. When I moved in 2009, I registered Libertarian.

Some may say that gay marriage is a wedge issue; however, gay marriage is just an example of individuals exercising their Constitutional rights. If a candidate does not believe in gay marriage, they do not believe in freedom. The 14th Amendment states that no state in the union can provide benefits to one group of people and not another. Gay marriage as a political issue has never been about forcing churches or private organizations to marry gays and lesbians. The political issue of gay marriage is about allowing citizens to exercise their Constitutional rights. Allowing citizens to vote on whether a group of people can exercise these rights goes against everything America should stand for—freedom.

My decision to leave the Left and become a libertarian had everything to do with freedom. I believe that Americans should have the right to exercise their economic and social freedoms as outlined by the Constitution. Citizens should have the right to run a business without government regulation. Taxes must be lowered and the deficit significantly reduced to ensure America's future prosperity. Personal beliefs regarding sexual orientation or business should not enter in to government's role in protecting and ensuring our freedoms. The right to religion should not impede someone's right to not be religious and refrain from following religious dogma. Government should not put restrictions on business or the social lives of citizens and the Libertarian Party is the only party that wants to ensure every American citizen's right to freedom regardless of personal beliefs.

I am proud to be a libertarian. I am happy that I broke free from the corrupt two-party system. I only wish more would follow. So many of my friends and family match the Libertarian Party's belief system more than the Democratic or Republican Parties they belong to. However, they are still trapped in that two-party system, believing their vote will not count for anything if they vote their conscience. My hope for America is that one day we will stop allowing the media to decide which candidates we get to choose, which candidates we get information on, and that candidates with the most campaign money will stop being our only choices. Even better, I hope that one day America will get rid of the party system altogether, that citizens will stop being labeled by their political party, and that candidates will be referred to as our fellow Americans. For now, leaving the Left and being a libertarian is a label I am proud to wear.

Elliot Engstrom
Law Student at the University of Georgia School of Law;
Athens, GA

Born and raised in Charlotte, North Carolina, Elliot Engstrom is a 2010 graduate of Wake Forest University and a member of the University of Georgia School of Law class of 2013. Elliot is an active member of both Young Americans for Liberty and the Federalist Society, and has written extensively for the Young Americans for Liberty blog, the *Old Gold & Black*, *Young American Revolution*, and *The Daily Caller*. His interests include sports of all kinds, philosophy, cooking, and French culture. In his free time he is most likely to be found at a bar watching his favorite soccer teams, Olympique de Marseille and Arsenal. He can be reached by e-mail at engstrom.elliot@gmail.com.

Oedipus Laevus
by
Elliot Engstrom

"Where a man absorbed in the effect which is seen has not yet learned to discern those which are not seen, he gives way to his fatal habits, not only by inclination, but by calculation." Frederic Bastiat, *That Which is Seen, and That Which is Not Seen*, 1850.

Some of the greatest works of art ever created are the Greek tragedies of Sophocles. *Antigone*, *Oedipus Rex* and the like have entertained and captivated audiences and readers for literally thousands of years, and likely will continue to do so for thousands more. What made, and continues to make, the writings of Sophocles so compelling is one dramatic concept that he employed flawlessly—hubris.

Hubris can be thought of at a basic level as pride, but it is more than that. It is pride that is so excessive, so overpowering, that it results in its possessor completing losing touch with reality. And, when dealing with hubris, there almost always are dire consequences as a result of one's blind arrogance.

In the greatest tragedies, the characters that meet their downfall by their own hands almost always have the best of intentions. Oedipus flees Corinth in a genuine effort to avoid killing his father and sleeping with his mother. However, the fact that his efforts are genuine did not change the fact that he was poorly informed about his situation, and therefore his actions had unintended consequences.

While I was raised in a fairly conservative household, I, like many others, did not truly begin to form my political beliefs until my college years. For my first several years at Wake Forest University, I became more and more aware of problems in our world that I never before knew existed. Billions of people on our planet live in poverty. The global environment is being ravaged by pollution, with species going extinct every day. Politicians and special interests are pushing the fragile international community ever closer to some form of global military conflict.

In the build-up to the 2008 election cycle, with these problems fresh in my mind, I was very impressed with then-Senator Barack Obama. It seemed difficult to say that he was wrong about his hope for the world. Who doesn't want less poverty and more prosperity? Who doesn't think that we need to take care of our nation's poor? Who in their right mind could possibly want to protect the super-rich at the expense of the common man? In my mind, to disagree with this man, you had to disagree with what he stood for, and that just seemed utterly ridiculous. I simply could not disagree with Senator Obama, because the things he wanted were the things I wanted.

However, I clearly am no longer a leftist. So what happened? Did my hopes for the world change? The answer is a resounding "no."

In the autumn of 2008, I went to study abroad in Dijon, France for a semester. I since have also spent time working in Aix-en-Provence, and in addition I majored in French in college and speak the language almost fluently. Needless to say, I love France and everything French, from the people to the cuisine to the culture.

However, my love for France does not mean that I ignore the realities of the many problems facing the European power. In fact, it was my time in France that inspired me to begin investigating why a country like France, that seemed to care for its poor and provide for the masses even more so than the United States, was having such widespread problems economically. What I found was that attempts to intervene in the economy to protect society's most vulnerable, while well intentioned, almost always result in massive unintended costs that outweigh the benefits of such action.

If I had to sum up in one word why I have abandoned people like now-President Barack Obama and the rest of the American Left, it is their hubris. It exists in many forms throughout the standard liberal spectrum, but I have come to see it more and more as the years have progressed. The first example that comes to mind is the government official who thinks that if he could just be given more control, he could make the necessary changes and plan peoples' lives for them, serving the common good at the end of the day.

However, this is not the leftist hubris that pushed me away from modern liberalism. Rather, for me it was the naïve college student who just did not understand why anyone should ever make more than $250,000, the English professor who thought that economics is a field of study for people who only care about money, and the social worker who thought that it was an affront to humanity to say anyone's labor could ever be worth less than the minimum wage. I was driven away from the Left by a political philosophy that turned up its nose at anyone who was willing to base their economic and political philosophy on one basic truth—every single human being is, at the end of the day, self-interested.

Perhaps the reason that many on the Left, including my former self, find this concept so despicable is that they immediately think of self-interest in its worst possible form—unbridled, all-encompassing greed. Granted, there are people like this in the world—arguably a very small minority. But not everyone's self-interest takes this form. In fact, one could just as easily say that the altruistic Left is as selfish as any other political viewpoint, as "selfishness is not living as one wishes to live, it is asking others to live as one wishes to live."[1]

When I encounter leftists with whom I disagree on social policy issues in particular, I find they often immediately jump to the conclusion that since I disagree with their means I necessarily disagree with their ends. Granted, if the end they have in mind is a world of forced economic equality, then I certainly do disagree with that end. However, I do not think that for most compassionate leftists in the United States the laws and regulations for which they campaign are ends in themselves. Rather, they are means meant to achieve the end of a better world for everyone. The fact that I do not agree with these means does not mean that I want more homeless people on the streets, just like the fact that I am against invading countries all over the world does not mean that I want a more vulnerable and endangered America.

Like the honest leftist, I want a world with less poverty. I want a world where food is affordable. I want a world with less war. I want a world where everyone can have a fulfilling job. My difference with the leftist is not on whether these are worthy ends, but rather on how to achieve these ends. The leftists' hubris truly starts to come into play when one sees that their means not only fail to achieve their goals, but also directly antagonize them. And yet, there is no reconsideration of how to act, no thought that maybe the American Left's public policy is based in misguided wishful thinking. Rather, the exact same policies are tried again, just on a grander scale, and these same policies once again fail.

Take the example of interest rates. Despite all of the talk in the news of how they are set by the Federal Reserve, interest rates exist independent of any government action. This is because an interest rate is essentially the price of money, and money itself is a naturally occurring phenomenon that has been monopolized by the State. Like any price, an interest rate is in constant flux. Unlike many prices, however, the price of money has a massive and direct effect on almost everything we do in our daily lives. For this reason, "public opinion always wants easy money, that is, low interest rates."[2]

The fact that I am against unnaturally low interest rates does not mean that I am against giving everyone easy access to money, or that I think that borrowing should be difficult for common people. It simply means that I recognize the devastating unintended consequences that result from artificial manipulation of interest rates. Like any price, an interest rate is a signal, and a false interest rate sends a false signal.

An interest rate, like gravity, is a natural occurrence. If a friend of mine were to attempt to jump over a canyon, and I told him that I would just lower gravity for him so that he could do it, he would not make it across. Rather, he would fall and die. This does not mean that someone who counseled me against attempting to lower gravity is against my friend making it across the canyon. It simply means that they are willing to accept reality, and work within its confines.

When interest rates are lowered, people borrow more money that they normally would. They then spend this money in an attempt to further their own personal fortunes. They might start a small business, buy a house, or invest in a construction project. Things are good for a little while. But then it comes time to repay the debts of the past, and since there was no increase in capital to accompany the increase in the

105

money supply that lowered interest rates, things begin to fall apart. This is one of several factors that have been crucially involved in every single major economic collapse in our nation during the past century.

However, the lesson here is not about interest rates, as a thorough discussion of money and the Federal Reserve is well beyond the bounds of this writing. The lesson, rather, is about intervention and unintended consequences. The American Left has developed a faith in the ability of government to fix our problems. If legislation is named the "Help the Poor People Act of 2011," attempts to push it through will be based merely on its name, and opposition to it will be met with accusations that "you just don't want to help the poor people." While this obviously is a bit of hyperbole, it is not that far from the truth, and the extent to which the modern American Left will go to deny economic reality is becoming more and more disturbing.

Take the example of Agriculture Secretary Tom Vilsack, who said that food stamps are an example of "the most direct stimulus you can get in the economy during these tough times."[3] Well, food stamps generate prosperity, right? "It's putting people to work. If people are able to buy a little more in the grocery store, someone has to stock it, package it, shelve it, process it, ship it. All of those are jobs."

Secretary Vilsack and many of his cohorts on both the Left and the Right continue to espouse an economic theory that has been repeatedly debunked for over 150 years. The reason is that men like Vilsack cannot respond to this question posed by Frederic Bastiat in 1850—if work of any sort in and of itself produces prosperity, then why don't we just pass out bats, have people run around breaking windows, and then pay someone else to go around and fix all of the broken glass?

Bastiat's answer is simple: "Your theory," he says, "is confined to that which is seen; it takes no account of that which is not seen . . . It is not seen that as our shopkeeper has spent six francs upon one thing, he cannot spend them upon another. It is not seen that if he had not had a window to replace, he would, perhaps, have replaced his old shoes, or added another book to his library. In short, he would have employed his six francs in some other way, which this accident has prevented."[4]

Oedipus knew that there was a problem that needed to be fixed. He knew that he needed to evade the possibility of killing his father and sleeping with his mother. However, as Oedipus's tragic tale shows, the fact that there is a problem does not justify the use of any solution. Trying to fix a problem without fully understanding it can result in dire consequences, and despite the fact that Oedipus put forth a genuine effort to avoid his fate, his lack of situational awareness drove him right to the place he never wanted to be.

Many on the Left have good intentions. However, good intentions are not enough to bring about good results in and of themselves. The worst part it is that many on the Left believe themselves to be superior simply because of their good intentions. This is hubris in its purest form. It is a hubris that is based in the leftists' inability to accept many of the basic realities of the world around them, and it is a hubris that has driven our country into an economic pit. It was the realization that this hubris exists throughout the American Left that led me to walk away from this political viewpoint.

My goal is not merely to chide those on the Left, but rather to ask them to wake up. If you really want a world with more affordable food, then study how food prices work in the marketplace instead of throwing government subsidies towards farmers. If you really want a world where there are less poor people, then try to genuinely understand the root causes of poverty, not just raise the minimum wage and increase welfare benefits. Good intentions are a good start. But they are not enough. Without more, good intentions can become hubris, and they will continue to send our country into an economic situation from which it becomes harder and harder to emerge. Without more, good intentions become an evil. As C.S. Lewis wrote, "of all tyrannies, a tyranny exercised for the good of its victims may be the most oppressive . . . those who torment us for our own good will torment us without end, for they do so with the approval of their conscience."[5]

End Notes

1.   Wilde, Oscar. *The Soul of Man under Socialism and Selected Critical Prose*. Ed. Linda C. Dowling. London: Penguin. 2001.

2.   Von Mises, Ludwig. *Critique of Interventionism*. Irvington-on-Hudson, NY: Foundation for Economic Education. 1996.

3.   "Obama Ag Secretary Vilsack: Food Stamps Are a Stimulus." RealClearPolitics. *RealClearPolitics—Opinion, News, Analysis, Videos and Polls*. Web. December 8, 2011. http://www.realclearpolitics.com/video/2011/08/16/obama_ag_secretary_vilsack_food_stamps_are_a_stimulus.html.

4.   Bastiat, Frédéric, and George B. De Huszar. *Selected Essays on Political Economy*. Irving-on-Hudson: Foundation For Economic Education. 1968.

5.   Lewis, C. S. *God in the Dock: Essays on Theology and Ethics*. Grand Rapids, MI: William B. Erdmans.1995.

Tom Garrison
Writer; St. George, UT

I am the youngest of four children to two Dust Bowl Okies who migrated to Shafter, CA in the Central Valley. My family was fairly apolitical, with Republican leanings. I graduated with a BA in political science (magna cum laude) from California State College, Bakersfield in 1974; earned a MA in political science from University of California, Davis in 1976; and finished everything but my PhD dissertation in political science (ABD) at University of California, Santa Barbara in 1980.

For 15 years I had a "career" (along with a full time job editing a political science journal) as a democratic socialist in Santa Barbara, CA. I began political life as a typical McGovern liberal, moved left to become a card carrying member of the Socialist Party USA, and in the late 1990s evolved into a libertarian.

During undergraduate and graduate studies I was active in-on campus politics. In 1980 I was arrested, along with hundreds of others, for civil disobedience at the Diablo Canyon nuclear power plant. From the early 1980s to the mid 1990s I was a hyper-active socialist: twice running for Santa Barbara City Council openly as a socialist in the mid-1980s; working with tenants, and gays and lesbians for years; and fighting political cultists in California's Peace and Freedom Party (the only socialist party with ballot status in California).

By the end of the '90s I embraced libertarianism. I now live in semi-retirement in St. George, Utah with my wonderful wife, Deb Looker, and our two cats, Dave and Molly.

Why I Left the Left*
by
Tom Garrison

"Point of racism."

Along with the ever popular "point of sexism," these additions to Roberts Rules of Order often echoed at statewide meetings of the California Peace and Freedom Party (PFP). You have to understand that one would be hard pressed to find a group less imbued with racist or sexist thoughts or behaviors than the leadership of the California Peace and Freedom Party—the only avowedly socialist party with ballot status in California. Yet, during debate members of some factions would often challenge any speaker who even mildly criticized or challenged the ideas of a person of color or woman by shouting "point of racism" and/or "point of sexism." Leftist democracy in action—try and intimidate your opponents by labeling them as racists and/or sexists. It is important to know that these folks are hypersensitive about race and sex and calling them racist or sexist is a powerful tool. It sounds ridiculous now and was silly then.

As a member of the PFP State Central Committee, I experienced these activities many times from the mid-1980s to the early 1990s. These were only a minor, and somewhat amusing, sidelight to the major themes of why I left the Left.

Basically there are four characteristics of the Left that made it impossible to continue with my leftist affiliations. I'll mix personal observations with a wider analysis and empirical evidence. The four characteristics are: <u>(1) a lack of respect for and understanding of the concept of personal responsibility for one's own actions; (2) unnecessary lying that undermined the democratic process; (3) a slavish adherence to "affirmative action" preferences, quotas, identity politics, and multicultural "diversity"; (4) and a strong intolerance for real diversity of ideas.</u>

As time went on, I found myself more and more at the non-leftist part of the political continuum. While not the only issues that split me from the Left, there are representative of how the Left (and contemporary liberals in general) just don't get it.

Personal Responsibility

Our local Socialist Party/PFP chapter had a meeting soon after the April 1992 riots in Los Angeles that followed the original Simi Valley trial and acquittal of the Los Angeles police officers who were charged with attacking Rodney King. As you recall, during those riots, a white truck driver, Reginald Denny, was savagely attacked by several black men for no reason other than that Denny was a white man in the wrong place at the wrong time. Damian Williams, of the "71 Hustlers" a prime attacker of Denny, used a piece of concrete to fracture Denny's skull in 91 places. Williams also did the "revolutionary" act of pulling down the pants of another unconscious white victim and spray-painting his genitals black while a mob watched and laughed[1] Even though Williams' actions were captured on videotape, he was later acquitted of the most serious charges.[2]

At our meeting one member proclaimed that we need to understand the black thugs (not their words) who attacked Denny and to see that their actions were not their fault but rather a function of societal oppression. Incredible! These thugs attack a totally innocent white man and we're supposed to tolerate it because the attackers are black. In our present culture feelings trump behavior.

Look at the facts. Damian Williams had a long history of gang-related violence. He could clearly make a choice between attacking a white man with whom he had no grudge and not attacking—the choice was his. But at least one member (and most likely several other sympathizers) of our local socialist group accepted and advanced the idea that poor Damian Williams was not to blame for his purposeful and vicious attack on a truly innocent victim who happened to be white. Society made him do it. Amazing.

Another very popular and obvious example of dismissing personal responsibility is the fairly recent idea of classifying alcoholism as a disease. Come on. If you believe that, then it is the only disease to have ever been eradicated by willpower. Quitting may be a difficult process, but an alcoholic can end his "disease" by simply *choosing* not to drink. That is, taking responsibility for his actions and not drinking.

If this were not the case, how else could we explain the millions of former alcoholics who simply choose not to drink and don't? Does their "disease" simply go away? In a sense yes, it does, once they decide to display some willpower and character.

It may be true that some folks have a genetic predisposition toward alcoholism. But that just means that once they know this, they should not drink. Abstaining may not be easy and requires willpower, but that certainly does not mean alcoholism is a disease.

However, the Left and liberals do seem to strongly latch on to any excuse for why an individual's crappy behavior is not his fault. Usually the mantra is that society is to blame. In this case, it is the mythical "disease" of alcoholism. Why is so difficult for leftists/liberals to simply say that someone does not have much character and/or willpower and this leads them to abuse alcohol. The answer is obvious—once the way is open to honestly discuss personal failing as a reason for destructive behavior, then other personal failings may also be attributed to an individual's own actions and not the fault of society. The whole underpinning of the Left and liberalism would be badly shaken. Leftism/liberalism relies on the proposition that, for the most part, people do not control their own lives and they need the government (for liberals) or the new socialist society (for leftists) to protect and watch out for them—the nanny state.

It is true society plays a role in molding people and that a black person in a racist society may face problems not of his own making. But contemporary America is not oppressively racist and there are plenty of chances for any hard working person who makes thoughtful choices to carve out a decent life. However, leftists/liberals are thoroughly immersed in the narcissism of minor differences. Noted civil rights activist Dr. James Meredith points out that:

> ... somewhere along the line, someone in power decided that the proud black race, a people who build cultures in Africa and built many of the physical structures of this nation, could not survive without a host of federal programs and giveaways.... A "dependency mentality" was created and fostered by black and white liberals looking to buy power. ... I have come to realize that while white racism exists, our

main roadblocks in the '90s are ones that have been created by our own so-called leadership.[3]

The situation today—approximately 40 percent of Americans receive federal government handouts of cash and valuable benefits (more than 45 million receive food stamps), financed by the 50 percent of citizens who actually pay taxes—further undermines personal responsibility. Assuming some percentage those receiving handouts are in a bad situation through no fault of their own, our nanny state system—fully supported by liberals and leftists—still enables tens of millions of Americans (and who knows exactly how many illegal aliens) to abrogate personal responsibility. The sad reality is that decades into the welfare/nanny state, virtually nothing has changed. According to political scientist and authority on public administration James Wilson:

> ...there are three simple behavioral rules for avoiding poverty: finish high school, produce no children before marrying, and no child before age 20. Only 8 percent of families who conform to all three rules are poor; 79 percent of those who do not conform are poor.[4]

All three rules are dependent upon personal responsibility. Act responsibly and your chances of living in poverty plummet. Individual responsibility, not society, is the key. Ask your favorite leftist/liberal if they agree and you will get a litany of "reasons" why people are victims of society, corporations, the rich, or some other boogeyman—anything but personal responsibility. After all, a villain is needed to justify the security blanket of the nanny state.

Unnecessary Leftist/Liberal Lying

During the 1980s my wife, Deb, and I were very active in the local Santa Barbara Tenants Union (SBTU). Other than our local socialist group, the Tenants Union was the most active "progressive" organization in Santa Barbara at that time.

At least some of the SBTU's permanent leadership (they always held office in the SBTU) were affiliated with the League of Revolutionary Struggle (LRS), a nationwide communist organization formed in 1978. The LRS considered itself anti-revisionist and took

114

inspiration from the Communist Party of China and its leader Mao Zedong. It was heavily invested in racial and ethnic identity politics.

How could we tell they were commies? The LRS published a newspaper called *Unity*. Even for a lefty paper it was pretty bad—full of slogans and stories of struggle against capitalism by just about anybody as long as they were non-white. By this time I was fairly well connected with the local reds, some LRS people and a few Revolutionary Communist Party (RCP) types. The only people who sold *Unity* were members of the SBTU's permanent leadership. When Deb and I asked if they were LRS members the reply was always, "I am a supporter of the *Unity* newspaper." Come on. Nobody except a dues-paying LRS member would try to sell that rag.

Deb and I had no problem with commies. Well, maybe a little problem with the fact that they were Marxists-Leninists and believed in the dictatorship of the proletariat. I had some concern that, if they were honest, they would most likely initiate violence (as opposed to self-defense) to achieve their ends. Ohhhh, and we had maybe a tinsy problem with the most likely outcome if their kind gained power—that people like Deb and I would be some of the first to be lined up against a wall and shot. Other than those small caveats, we were fine with the local commies.

But this transparent lying about their political affiliation means that when the "revolution" comes it will be led in Santa Barbara by political activists who are, if not skilled at lying, at least comfortable with it. A great start for a new humanistic order.

Lying about one's principal political affiliation has a long history on the Left. There may have been justification for underground political work (including lying about leftist political affiliations) in Czarist Russia or 1980s El Salvador. But in 1980s America?

I twice ran for Santa Barbara City Council (1985 and 1987) openly as a socialist. In several years (early 1980s to mid-1990s) of very intense political activity—all of it done openly as a member of the California Peace and Freedom Party and the Socialist Party, USA—I never had a major hassle with the public due to being a socialist and promoting socialism. Neither did any of the score or so core members of our local socialist group.

Keep in mind that this was the apogee of the Reagan-Bush years and I was doing openly socialist political work in Ronald Reagan's adopted home town. As a matter of fact, I think my campaigns and other political work by myself and others in our local socialist group greatly benefited from our honesty and being a novelty. I was treated fairly and with respect by moderates and conservatives and the local media. I had dozens of intense yet civil discussions with capitalists and other running dogs.

The only real problems came from liberals who wanted me to lie and say I was simply another "progressive" Democrat—a stupid idea for several reasons. "Progressive"/liberal Democrats are a dime a dozen in Santa Barbara. At least one runs for every office in the county. I was not a Democrat and was not about to lie concerning my basic political affiliations, even though I surly would have received more votes if I did. But it would have been a betrayal of the public trust and my own values. It still seems odd that Democratic Party activists encouraged me to lie.

During both campaigns my campaign literature noted my membership in the Socialist Party and the Peace and Freedom Party—I ran openly as a socialist. What is the use of being a socialist and not openly pushing it? A socialist running as a "progressive" or liberal Democrat is simply one more liberal Democrat and does not advance the democratic socialist "revolution" in any meaningful manner. If nothing else, my running openly as a socialist showed people who met me during the campaign that a "red" could also be a thoughtful believer in democracy (and they could see that I did not have horns).

"Affirmative Action" Preferences, Identity Politics, and Multicultural "Diversity"

My campaigns were run by committees of decent hard working leftists. I still have nothing but admiration for almost all who were at the center of the campaigns. Among many interesting discussions during my two campaigns for Santa Barbara City Council was one that emerged in both campaigns and demonstrates illogical pandering to the god of multicultural "diversity" and identity politics.

To become a US citizen, one must demonstrate competence in the English language. My campaign committees had serious discussions about whether or not to print some of our campaign literature in Spanish. Many felt that doing so would help us gain the Latino vote. (More than one-third of the population in Santa Barbara is of Hispanic ancestry.)

My wife and I consistently argued that since only citizens could register to vote, and since naturalized Hispanic citizens must have competence in the English language (or they could not become citizens), there was no need for Spanish language campaign material. Those not competent in English could not become citizens and, thus, could not vote. Further, since virtually all Hispanic-ancestry citizens born in the US would speak English by the time they could register to vote, there was absolutely no need for Spanish language campaign material.

Our logic won the day, but it interesting that the folks working in my campaigns would even broach this subject in a serious manner. Their arguments demonstrated the power of multiculturalism and the need of the Left to pander to identity politics.

Like most communist groups, the LRS was active in the Democrat Party (although not always openly as LRS members). Nationally they played an important role in the Rainbow Coalition and the 1984 and 1988 campaigns to elect Jesse Jackson as president.

The LRS folks and their supporters also exhibited an incredible ability to politically support almost anyone—excepting, of course, the most blatant conservative—as long as that person had black or brown skin and was a Democrat.

They demonstrated this behavior when Democrat Tom Bradley, a black moderate (at best), ran for governor of California in 1986. Other than being black, Bradley had almost no progressive/leftist credentials. The Tenants Union had a radical constitution and, as noted above, some members of the leadership were LRS members. My wife and I, being serious and open leftists, argued strenuously that the Tenants Union should endorse the PFP candidate (a Hispanic woman, Maria Elizabeth Munoz) instead of the milquetoast Bradley for governor. While we managed to convince several Tenants Union members who were not LRS "supporters" to endorse the true leftist candidate, the majority voted to endorse Bradley (the vote was 13 to seven for Bradley).

Understand the underlying political context. An endorsement by the Santa Barbara Tenants Union for any candidate for statewide office would only influence at most a couple of hundred voters in Santa Barbara—almost certainly not enough to make a difference for any candidate. But, by openly backing a socialist (the PFP candidate) the organization would help build a base outside the Democrat Party for progressives and leftists. On the other hand, backing a tired old moderate Democrat would mean almost nothing and build little except allegiance to what almost everyone in the leadership agreed was a corrupt Democrat Party. Moreover, it would show that the Tenants Union supported a black male candidate over a Hispanic woman. It didn't matter that Bradley would offer at best lukewarm support for the goals of the Tenants Union, while the PFP candidate would whole heartedly support those goals. Bradley was a black Democrat—that was enough. A clear example of identity politics wining over issue-based ideological politics.

One of the most impressive examples of identity politics and race pandering was the hoopla surrounding the June 29, 1995 US Supreme Court decision (a five to four vote) ordering the state of Georgia to redraw its 11th Congressional District in a manner that omits race as the "predominant" factor. Subsequent redistricting of five "racially gerrymandered" black-majority Congressional districts into white-majority districts in Florida, Georgia, and Texas spurred leftists, liberals, and so-called black leaders to predict (read their words) Armageddon for black folks in America.

The ruling was "the first step in the resegregation of American electoral democracy," according to Wade Henderson, legal director of the National Association for the Advancement of Colored People (NAACP). He added "If race can't be a factor, it's going to be almost impossible to preserve these black districts"[5]. Cynthia McKinney, the black female Democrat incumbent in Georgia's 11th district, lamented the ruling as "...a setback for democracy" and said that she believed that "The issue of fairness has been squarely left behind"[6]. That paragon of virtue President Clinton called the decision a "setback in the struggle to ensure that all Americas participate fully in the electoral process"[7]. And Rev. Jesse Jackson said this limit on racial gerrymandering would produce an "ethnic cleansing of Congress."[8]

Guess what? The sky did not fall and black folks are not once again in slavery. All five black incumbents in the former black-majority and now white-majority Southern districts won their races in the November 1996 Congressional elections. Maybe Americans, even white Southerners, are not as racist as identity politics leaders would have us believe.

By early 1996 I had become fed up with affirmative action preferences and quotas in government, college admissions, etc. I took a small, entirely unscientific, survey to gather empirical evidence as to the extent of discrimination against women in college and the workplace. Over a couple of months, I asked co-workers and friends if they had ever been discriminated against in school or the workplace because of their sex. I polled nine women, from their early 20s to their late 40s, if they felt they had suffered sexual discrimination at any point during the last ten years. (I used ten years because I figured that even the most retrograde men had at least heard of sexual discrimination by the mid-1980s and knew that it was unacceptable and could be illegal.) None, that's correct *none*, of the respondents reported *any* discrimination based on their sex.

Of course, the sample was small and my method unscientific. But if sexual discrimination was as rampant as leftists and feminists would have us believe, I figured at least half the women I talked to would report some sexual discrimination in the past decade. And if we are to believe feminists and the advocates of preferences and quotas, it is damn near impossible that not one of the nine women had been a victim of sexual discrimination.

I know sexual discrimination exists. But from my own observations, questioning, and much reading, I cannot believe that it is anywhere as pervasive as feminists and quota advocates would have us believe. Perhaps they need to keep "victimhood" alive to maintain their own jobs in Women's Studies programs and the cottage industry of sexual discrimination.

In a March 23, 1998 *Newsweek* essay Meg Greenfield clearly stated the major problem with identity politics (and by extension support of affirmative action preferences, quotas, and multiculturalism):

> To let yourself be transformed into the emblem of some cause, any cause, or demographic category, and to draw your identity and take your marching orders from it is to kick away your freedom, your independence and your individuality. It is to suspend all these and basically to lose your influence over events that matter to you. You will find you have forgotten how to speak out with views that do not conform to those of the group or that you will have been led not to trust such views. You will see life through a very narrow lens and be very much in the control of those who do the defining of the group interest.[9]

Intolerance for True Diversity of Ideas

Several years ago my wife and I got into a political discussion with another couple while on a trip to Las Vegas. While cruising sin city in our rental car, I remember relating how I have two good friends who are conservative—two undergraduate teachers with whom I still maintain contact after graduating decades ago. The guy, let's call him Mr. N, replied that he had never met a conservative who he believed was not a fascist in disguise. No matter what I said, Mr. N would not accept the idea that a conservative could be principled and decent person—that there exists such an animal as a Burkian conservative who is not racist, not sexist, not anti-democratic, but simply has an ideology that challenges many tenants of modern liberalism.

I encountered the same or similar attitude dozens of times with leftists and liberals, albeit usually in not such an unvarnished manner. The truly unfortunate thing is that I doubt if Mr. N ever had a serious discussion with a principled conservative. It might lead to some doubt and the notion that a conservative could be seen as a real person and not simply a stereotype.

It was a bit of a shock to realize that Mr. N—while not a leftist but a strong liberal—could not accept as valid the idea that there exist people of good will who were not of his political persuasion. He was clearly being intolerant of other political views. I realized that the much touted diversity of the last 35 years or so does not seem to include the most meaningful type of diversity—a diversity of ideas.

Years ago I came across an interesting article in *The Wall Street Journal* that reported on a study at the University of Colorado and academic tolerance, or lack thereof. It is the premier public university in a state in which registered Republicans (at that time) outnumber Democrats by more than 100,000—a state in which the Republican Party controlled both houses of the state legislature from the mid-1970s to the mid-1990s. The article noted that in 13 social science and humanities departments at the University's main campus in Boulder, Democrats outnumbered Republicans by a ratio of 31 to one. Of the 190 professors affiliated with a political party 184 were Democrats. Not a single Republican turned up in major departments such as English (29 Democrats) and psychology (20 Democrats). There was a single Republican in anthropology (10 Democrats), education (21 Democrats), sociology (12 Democrats), and two Republicans in political science (14 Democrats).[10] Students could easily go through four years of "liberal" education without taking a social science or humanities class from a single Republican professor. Students find themselves in an environment in which liberal professors don't merely dominate the faculty, they essentially are the faculty.

A more recent study in 2005 and reported in the *Washington Post* by Howard Kurtz finds similar results from a survey of 1,643 fulltime college faculty across the country. By their own description, 72% of those teaching at American colleges and universities are liberal and 15% are conservative. At elite schools, the disparity is more pronounced—87% of the faculty is liberal and 13% conservative[11]. These are only two of several studies that reach the same conclusion.

This ideological hegemony is the obvious result of diversity that only takes race/ethnicity and gender into consideration. What happened to the idea that an undergraduate education was intended to provide diverse ideological stimuli and produce graduates who are able to think critically about a range of subjects? Unfortunately, as other studies show, the University of Colorado at Boulder is not an anomaly in its slavish adherence to a very narrow notion of diversity. How is this ideological bias different in method and result from McCarthyism of the 1950s?

I personally experienced ideological intimidation during the Proposition 187 campaign (1994) and its aftermath. The proposition was designed to deny state welfare benefits to illegal immigrants. (On November 8, 1994 it passed 59% to 41 %.) I wrote a couple of letters to the editor and an opinion essay that were published in local newspapers.[12] Of course, some local liberals replied and in print I was referred to as mean-spirited and probably racist. In addition, a couple of friends refused to take my arguments seriously, and publicly derided me for questioning the Left/liberal belief that America is an open house with complete benefits for anyone who can sneak over the border. All this over some published letters and essays that were replete with logic and facts.

This questioning of the condition of my spirit and my supposed racism would seem very odd for anyone who knows my history—like the fact that in the preceding 15 years I had voted for, given money to, and publicly worked in electoral campaigns wherein 70 to 80% of the candidates were brown or black and most often women. Yes, I certainly have a history of racism.

But then facts are not the point, the point is to threaten people with vile labels if they overstep the bounds of politically correct thought. Yet another clear example of intolerance for true diversity.

Conclusion

Around this time, the mid- to late 1990s, I began to reconsider my commitment to socialism. I, and most of Santa Barbara socialist group, advocated New Left decentralized power. Marx's idea of the withering away of the state and voluntary cooperation among empowered citizens was our goal and guideline for action. For me, accepting free markets was simply applying my end state to current actions. And since I was always a Libertarian on social issues—such things as supporting gay rights, pro-choice, gun ownership via the 2nd Amendment, legalizing personal drug use—the evolution into a classical liberal/libertarian was not as drastic as one may think. As I began to read libertarian thinkers and magazines (*Reason* and *Liberty*) I came to see that the decentralized aspects of New Left ideology fit well with free markets and free minds. By the late 1990s I considered myself a libertarian and joined the Libertarian Party.

I have not found the four characteristics discussed in this essay that typify leftism/liberalism in libertarianism. Libertarianism is founded on personal responsibility and limited government; while they probably exist, I have yet to encounter libertarians who practice political lying; affirmative action and identity politics are not, for libertarians, worshiped at the altar of political correctness; and Libertarians are a diverse group who are tolerant of ideological diversity.

The Left betrayed me. As a young man I eagerly read about the Left, Marxism, socialism, and leftist heroes. My understanding was that the Left was striving to create a society wherein people could fully use their talents and together create a true democratic society. It seemed obvious that taking responsibility for one's actions was a necessary part of the equation, as was being a stand-up citizen/activist by not engaging in political lying. Equally obvious was the need to end racism and sexism, but not by creating new systems where some folks are given extra consideration because of their skin tone or sex—a long-term recipe for polarization and divisiveness. I also expected the new society to display a real tolerance for a diversity of ideas. A crucial aspect in avoiding "thought police" that I then assumed was necessary, and still strongly believe is a keystone for a better society.

"To hold the same views at 40 as we held at 20 is to have been stupefied for a score of years."[13]

*This is a revised and updated version of an essay originally published in the January 2000 issue of *Liberty* magazine.

End Notes
1.   Caldwell, Christopher. "Anatomy of a Riot." *The Wall Street Journal*. February 2, 1998.

2.   Will, George F. "Official Negligence." *Newsweek*. February 16, 1998. p. 80.

3.   Meredith, James. "A Challenge to Change." *Newsweek*. October 6, 1997. p. 18.

4.   Will, George F. "A GI Bill for Mothers." *Newsweek*. December 22, 1997. p. 88.

5.   Muwakkil, Salim. "Down by Law." *In These Times*. July 24, 1995. p. 20.

6.   Muwakkil, Salim. "Down by Law." *In These Times*. July 24, 1995. p. 20.

7.   Barrett, Paul M. and Gerald Seib. "Supreme Court Redraws Political Battleground With Broad Attack on Race-Based House Districts." *The Wall Street Journal*. June 30, 1995. p. A16.

8.   Will, George F. "Decisiveness of Message Rather than Race." *Santa Barbara News-Press*. November 11, 1996.

9.   Greenfield, Meg. "Kicking Away Your Freedom." *Newsweek*. March 23, 1998. p. 76.

10.   Carroll, Vincent. "Republican Professors? Sure, There's One." *The Wall Street Journal*. May 11, 1998.

11.   Kurtz, Howard. "College Faculties A Most Liberal Lot, Study Finds." *Washington Post.com*. March 29, 2005. http://www.washingtonpost.com/wp-dyn/articles/A8427-2005Mar28.html.

12.   Garrison, Tom. "Rational discourse in discussing immigration." Essay. *Santa Barbara News-Press*. June 7, 1995. Garrison, Tom. "No Victims Allowed." Letter to the editor. *The Santa Barbara Independent*. July 27-August 3, 1995. Garrison, Tom. "Let's have reasoned debate on immigration issue." Letter to the editor. *Santa Barbara News-Press*. April 13, 1996.

13.   *Smithsonian*. September 1998. Volume 29, Number 6. p. 127.

Michelle A. C. Goodwin
Stay-at-home mom; Upton, MA

Michelle is currently a stay-at-home mom, living in central Massachusetts with her husband, Mike, and three children: Stephanie, Stanley, and Stacey. She earned a B.A. (summa cum laude) in Sociology from the University of Massachusetts, completing a thesis entitled "The Diffusion of Gifted Education in America."

Michelle's life has been committed to volunteerism and community service from her early years as a Missing Persons Recovery Specialist and Red Cross Disaster Volunteer to her current roles as a Cub Scout den leader, Daisy troop leader, Town Hall Renovation Committee Member, and most recent addition of Mendon-Upton Regional School Committee Member.

Michelle is fairly new to the Libertarian Party, learning about the party platform during Bob Barr's 2008 run for the presidency. She is currently registered as one of four Libertarians in the Town of Upton, Massachusetts, and was elected in May 2011 to a three-year term on the Mendon-Upton School Board. Michelle is looking forward to many more years of community service and activity with the Libertarian Party.

My Journey to Libertarianism
by
Michelle A. C. Goodwin

I was born in Massachusetts, raised in Massachusetts, and will probably die in Texas. Growing up I never heard of a Republican until this strange person, Ronald Reagan, was elected President in November 1980. I watched the inauguration at school. I grew up hearing how wonderful Democrats were, trying to help people and make sure that they could live the lives they wanted without the government telling them what to do. It was comforting to know that I would never be forced to have a certain lifestyle, career, or family. I heard frequently about the freedoms we were winning for blacks, women, gays, and so many others. It was a wonderful life, until I no longer fit in.

During my twenties I began to understand the idea that there are many perspectives to the same story. I was never comfortable with labeling people and judging them as friend or foe. Perhaps it was my recognition of how much I was misunderstood by others that allowed me to see that maybe the Republicans weren't really evil people from the uneducated south and Midwest. I began to learn that bigotry and prejudice can permeate our lives without ever knowing it just by the way the community around us speaks and behaves. When I moved west with my husband, all the way from Massachusetts to upstate New York, I started a true journey through political and social philosophy.

I began my time in Syracuse by trying to replicate my life "back home." I quickly found the true discomfort in living a life that was handed to me instead of one that represented my true self. I began to explore new religious ideas, new social ideas, and new political ideas. Why are there so many Jewish people here and can I send my daughter to their pre-school? Why is there a line here where a soda called Coke is suddenly replaced with a pop called Pepsi? Why are "educated" communities more likely to be Democrats and "religious" communities more likely to be Republican? And what happens when you have an educated religious community?

126

In Massachusetts it was clear that if one was educated, one didn't believe in the foolishness of God and Bible, "educated religious" was an oxymoron. So I grew up believing that the truly progressed people were the educated atheists. Everyone else was behind and it was our responsibility to help them to learn how their ways were wrong and could be corrected with appropriate education. It wasn't until I moved further west, to South Dakota, that I began to see the hypocrisy of the educated atheist groups as they scorned the "religious right" for claiming that they were right and were there to help everyone else learn how their ways were wrong. Right or Left, everyone saw only one side, and no one would allow the other to live in peace.

It was also in South Dakota where I experienced the parallel worlds of racial prejudice. Being one-fourth Native American, and having darker skin and hair and carved facial bone structure, the experienced Anglo community of western South Dakota could pick me out a mile away. When I walked through the streets there it was as if two worlds existed in the same place at the same time. White didn't see native, and native didn't see white. It wasn't co-existence. It was a defect in the space-time continuum. The physical effect of this racial divide was an excellent metaphor to the parallel worlds of the Democrats and Republicans. Both existed in the same space and time, but neither could see the other or interact. Truly not how I saw life as meant to be lived.

By the time we moved to Alaska I was pretty independent-minded. I knew what I believed and I wasn't going to join a party that didn't have a platform that worked for me. I believed in personal freedom. I didn't want the government to tell me how to live my life. I didn't want the government teaching me what to think, forcing me to pray, denying me rights or liberties because of my perceived status—judged by imperfect, bigoted, prejudiced, power-hungry, indifferent politicos. This brought me to the Democratic side at a time when our economy was great and Republicans were looking to alter our Constitution to deny rights instead of guarantee them.

As wars began and the economy wobbled the focus moved from legislating religious beliefs to legislating capitalism. I believed in personal freedom. I didn't believe the government should be telling people or companies how to spend their money, save their money, invest their money, sell their products, or even design and make their products. I believe in the power of supply and demand and the intelligence of the consumers to make educated decisions for themselves. If someone wants to buy a product that is potentially harmful to them, it's their right to do so. Who am I to say what is harmful to whom? We do not need regulated consumers, we need educated consumers.

And so by then I was leaning heavily to the Republican Party. I didn't like their social platform, I was adamantly against it. But I couldn't stand any further government reach and growth, and the Republicans seemed to be the only ones who might stop it. I was very disappointed when, under Bush, our government grew tremendously in the early twenty-first century. The bills piled up, but the taxes kept going down. And so the deficit grew while social freedoms eroded. We were losing on both sides.

When Bob Barr became the Libertarian Party presidential candidate in 2008, I decided to check him out. I was disgusted with both John McCain and Barack Obama. We needed to have a real option. It was the first time I learned about Libertarians and their platform. I was in disbelief that any political party could actually be a place for me. As a social liberal and fiscal super-conservative, it just seemed impossible. But I could fit in. There was a place for me at the table and I was happy to join. I have been a registered Libertarian ever since.

I left the Left because the radical takeover of personal responsibility by the government was something I could not tolerate. It was something I had to fight. The hatred of the Right created overwhelming tension and wasted energy on non-creative and combative actions. The unwillingness to work with all people, to see all sides closed doors of opportunity and frustrated any attempts for real progress. The extreme beliefs of socialism instead of capitalism punished the hard-working and entrepreneurial spirit of America.

Being a Libertarian is not being an extreme Republican. It's the ability to function in the middle ground of liberty, responsibility, and justice. The Left may argue they are the fighters in this regard, not the libertarians. But the Left fail because they are actually creating a society that tells you your liberties, takes away your responsibilities, and creates justice through equal and opposite injustice.

Libertarians give the power back to the individual, creating little need for government as the people regulate themselves. What libertarians have that the Left lack is trust. We trust in our Constitution and our people. If the Left trusted as well, they wouldn't be fighting for all the control. As a libertarian I am finally, truly, fighting for the freedom of our people. I take full responsibility for that. And in the end, justice will prevail.

Ashley Harrell
Substitute Teacher; Saginaw, MI

I am 24 years old. In 2009 I graduated from the University of Michigan at Flint with a BA degree in English. I currently work as a substitute teacher in Saginaw, Michigan. I joined the Michigan Libertarian Party in September of 2010. I write fiction and love reading Ayn Rand.

A Liberal Girl in a Federalist World
by
Ashley Harrell

I became a libertarian a few years after college. It was an exciting transition because libertarianism outlines a clear, logical philosophy that is simple yet challenging to apply to most issues. Two key things happened that showed me libertarianism was the best answer. First, I saw how strong central government came burdened with horrible, predictable problems. Second, I saw the light, the truth of libertarianism.

I started as liberal as they come. Even as a young girl, I was outspoken and unequivocal about what I believed was right, dominated by my compassion for others. As far back as I can remember I was at odds with my family because I didn't harbor racist feelings, wasn't disturbed by gay people, and didn't blame the poor. They were conservative Republicans, and it was clear to me I was the opposite. I stereotyped myself into believing I was a liberal Democrat, and thanks to my family, I was a battle ready crusader. I debated every student at school, joined civil rights organizations, charities, signed petitions, and wrote letters, always to help people, always to aid the disenfranchised. I took this with me everywhere.

I went to college believing education is the key to freedom. In 2006 I graduated from Delta Community College and transferred to the University of Michigan at Flint. I pursued a liberal arts education. Growing up in a family of modest means, I saw that a happy life did not require a big paycheck, or lots of possessions. Reading *Walden* by Henry David Thoreau greatly inspired me that it was more valuable to live simply, with as little as possible, because then you don't have to spend all your time maintaining your possession. Here in America, a great life is available for very little money, and any job above minimum wage would be enough to get the things I needed.

Again, I was at odds with my family. Ever practical, my grandmother urged me toward engineering, science, or business, some field with great paying jobs. How could I get her to understand money has little value to me? Time is the most valuable possession any of us have, and I don't want to spend it pursuing a paycheck. People are the most important thing in the world, and I had to spend my time fighting, helping, and crusading for those who couldn't do it for themselves. I graduated in 2009, and entered a difficult job market. But thanks to President Obama, the stimulus, and the federal government, I found work to get me through difficult economic times. I thought it would be the perfect place for me, but instead I saw how federalism works in real life. It wasn't pretty.

My first post-graduation job was funded through the American Recovery and Reinvestment Act of 2009 (the "stimulus" bill). Say what you will, it got me through hard times. A non-profit agency hired me as a coordinator to help put together a program to for inner-city youth in Flint, Michigan. The program found summer jobs for them as part of the economic stimulus. Our particular grant catered to very specific applicants—those who met financial status requirements and had another barrier, like being a single parent, a high school dropout, or having a criminal history that could prevent them from being hired. As it may be in other American cities, Flint, Michigan (also Saginaw and Detroit) are desperate places, marred with poverty, illiteracy, drugs, and violence. A large portion of the population may be considered unemployable, dealing with such employment barriers as criminal history, illiteracy, or single parenthood. Our program's objective was to find 50 such young people, offer them training in work etiquette, resume writing, and job hunting, thus preparing them to enter the job market on their own. We were to explore what careers they wanted, and set them up with simple, entry-level jobs relating to their field. In addition, we gave them support and guidance through the summer, creating a successful first job experience to catapult them into their future. While ultimately I disagree with this program, it is attempting to address an issue that does need to be addressed. We cannot afford to ignore the large portion of the population that cannot read or get work. We cannot afford to let this problem go unsolved. However, expecting a federal program to help and support every city and town in America is ludicrous and having the federal government give money to businesses to hire people when the funds are unearned does not encourage personal responsibility in the applicants or the business.

From the beginning, it didn't work as planned. That isn't unusual, and we will leave Murphy's Law out of it. What disturbed me was apparent corruption. My job was to interview and hire the participants based on their qualifications. But once selection was started, I found half the spots already filled with kids of friends and acquaintances of the CEOs of my employers. I considered that this by itself wasn't really terrible because I knew how much Flint needed the program, if at least needy individuals were getting employment and a chance to learn to take care of themselves. But that wasn't the case.

Many of these youths didn't meet the requirements—they didn't have that additional barrier. But the director told me to find a way, to work it out, to get them in the system. Then it came time to place the applicants. We promised jobs that would aid in entering chosen careers. But the available jobs were lacking. Most participants wanted jobs in the medical field, but for one reason or another only one medical job was available. Again, the decision was out of my hands, the coveted spot going to a youth shoehorned in by his connections to the CEO of the non-profit agency. During the program, I got to know him, and soon admired his maturity, hard work, and strong morals. He certainly deserved his success. He took advantage of all his available opportunities—he'd even been to China. In the free market world this boy will have a better job than I ever could in no time flat.

But this program was designed to help young high school students who might not be able to graduate and ever find a job without major intervention. Even worse than this case, the director's stepson found a position in the program. The director felt this was fine since we didn't know he was a relative until after the program began. But again, problems arose when it came time for placement. The only prestigious position went to the stepson, the decision kept completely out of my hands—the system was abused.

As much as these injustices aggravated me, nothing compared to the eye-opening conversation I had with another employee. With a simple, sincere statement, she showed me the real problem with liberal, federal programs had nothing to do with greed or corruption—there is an attitude problem.

This young woman was about my age, motivated the same as I was to help people. The agency hired her to work on another federally funded program, one that aided very poor people with housing. The program provided funding for families for two years. The sadness and concern this young woman felt was palpable as she spoke to me. "These people will finally get decent housing, but the program only lasts two years. Then what? What does the government expect them to do?"

Flabbergasted, I struggled to understand what she was saying. She believed these people would never be able to take care of themselves, and must be coddled—not just for months, or for years, but forever. It was insulting. Two years is a very long time, long enough to find ways of self-support, long enough for a person to change his or her life. Here, I realized the true injustice all this federal spending added up to: dependence on the state.

Frankly, I grew weary of the Democratic Party when I realized they only pay lip service to the issues I care about. The party hasn't really done more than Republicans to help the poor, to let lesbian, gay, bisexual, and transgender families live the same as other families, or end the drug war. I thought that meant I would have to move farther left than mainstream Democrats. But seeing how tax dollars were so easily abused, misappropriated, and disrespected, I finally knew there was some power the government just wasn't meant to have. At first, my heart was torn. If the government wasn't going to help the poor, to bring up the disenfranchised, what would happen to them? Who would do it?

That's when I fell in love with the Libertarian Party, with liberty and the free market—the invisible hand that enables people to reach their potential, creates wealth, and promotes personal responsibility.

I first encountered the Libertarian Party in college. I was an active College Democrat and the College Libertarians were the most active political student group on campus. Obviously, we butted heads.

I had several personal disagreements with the College Libertarian president that left me with a nasty view of the party. But alas, he won my heart. Just before I graduated, the College Libertarians held a book fair. On a table lay dozens of books the club president promised would illuminate the error of my ways. What liberal could possibly say no to free books? He instructed me to choose any books I wanted, and I would receive my own copy in a few weeks. I looked carefully and selected several that interested me on a personal level: *1984* by George Orwell, *The Anti-Federalist Papers*, a book on the Roman Empire, and *Drug War Crimes: The Consequences of Prohibition* by Jeffrey A. Miron. All of these books left me with novel and exciting ideas but *Drug War Crimes* truly opened my eyes to the Libertarian Party. It illustrated so clearly how interfering with the free market by creating a prohibition created the single most destructive force in the drug war: a black market. I came to understand this the same time I saw the problems with government funding, and I learned the lesson I feel is the most important one the Libertarian Party can teach: our hearts can be wrong. My heart may tell me that drugs are bad and must be stopped at any cost, but in fact, the cost comes quickly and much too high, and there are better ways to deal with it. It may feel right to aid poor families with government programs, but that can also have serious consequences which can be worse than no help at all.

The government has an important job, but it is a limited one. It isn't the government that fights poverty, it's us. It's me. Libertarians never say don't help the poor, only that the government can't do it. I can do it. Libertarians never say don't fight for equality, only that the government is incapable of it. I am capable of it.

I still seek work where I can help people, without much thought about the paycheck. However, I now seek it in the free market, a place that existed before any civilized government, or political party. The free market will continue after everything we know has changed, an idea that will always serve the greatest benefit to the greatest number. I am a liberal Libertarian.

135

Lori Heine
Writer; Phoenix, AZ

At the age of two, she reportedly proclaimed, to a clerk at Goldwater's Department Store, that she was voting for the proprietor for president. It was too early in life for her to cast that ballot. She grew up at the tail end of the Baby Boomer generation, seduced by the promise that big government could guarantee the good life. But her inheritance, as part of that generation, also included the urge to question authority, to love freedom and to follow her heart and mind. She fell into the family business, insurance, and worked very hard to make a life for herself.

She came out as a lesbian, and in the fervor of membership in a new "community," swung hard to the Left. She voted for Barack Obama. But she has been unemployed since a month after his election. Hope and change, she has come to learn, are the products not of government regulation, but of freedom. A "closet" libertarian for several years, she has now "come out" yet again.

Lori found this second "coming out" as liberating as the first. She wishes it was not too late to vote for a different Barry—the one who would have brought real hope and change. She is dedicated, now,

136

to working for the transformation that can make this country, again, a beacon of freedom to the world. In that spirit, she has embarked on a career that allows her to follow her heart and mind: writing about the liberty she has learned to love. She still lives in Arizona, where she is single and enjoying the search for a life partner with whom she can share her dream.

The Undead
by
Lori Heine

We who have faithfully and trustingly supported the Left have been had. We are being scammed. The "hope and change" they offer us is nothing but an empty shell. And if we continue to follow them, we will end up empty shells instead of complete human beings.

Most rank-and-file leftists are not villains, nor are they idiots. Usually, they are good, kind, decent and sincere people. And they are being tricked. It's a hoax, a fraud—and a crime. One of the worst things about the leftist power-play is what it's doing to the good people who have placed their faith in the Left.

The Left depends upon disgruntled minorities for support. But to keep the support of minorities, like gays such as myself, it seems willing to do its own fair share to ensure that we remain disgruntled. We are supposed to remain forever scared, aggrieved, and outraged. That is what keeps us motivated and manipulated.

The worst thing isn't that the Left consistently makes promises on which it fails to deliver. It's that it seems to do things designed to work at cross purposes with its stated goals. In almost every instance, it ends up doing more harm to its core constituents instead of protecting them or improving their lot. Those who support the Left want to believe they are doing good for those they care about. But in actuality, they are doing them harm.

It is necessary to the Left that their rivals/partners on the Right continue to attack those under the leftist protectorate. Women, gays, people of color, and the poor must—*must*–be mistreated, so our "progressive" heroes can ride, again and again and again, to our rescue. Nothing seems to depress them more than the possibility that we might not be mistreated as much as they claim. They seem to fear nothing so much as the haunting possibility that we may no longer be victimized or oppressed.

People naturally desire to better their lives. No one wants to stay stuck in a bad situation. But those whose identity derives from wielding power and influence in the political process—the Left—must, at all costs, keep us there. It's the way to get us to keep following them.

The irony is that in order to hold government power, they must make us despair of ever enjoying personal power ourselves. If *they* are to move in and heavy-handedly control every aspect of our lives, then *we* must be kept from controlling our own lives. By all means, we must remain unaware of our own potential for grassroots power.

This is why the Tea Party, a ground-up movement without any top-heavy leadership, must never, in the statists' world, be allowed to survive.

The Right is stronger than the Left because—despite all the leftist hoopla about "diversity"—it is actually more diverse. For all its "power-to-the-people" pretensions, the Left has always been about big-government control. Conservatives have a strong libertarian tradition, and many of them have never forgotten this. Social conservatism, which is often little more than an immature, emotional reaction against leftist statism, has become what reactions always become—a mirror-image of what they oppose. The true hope of this country can be found in the fact that a growing number of people *do* remember an older, more robust tradition—one of individual self-reliance, of community that needs not be held together from above, and of principles whose truth shines forth for us to freely recognize rather than being crammed down our throats.

I still have the same core convictions I held as a leftist. I still truly believe in community, in cooperation that allows competition so we can hold each other accountable and help make each better. And in the inalienable rights of individuals, each of whom has intrinsic value in his or her own right. I believe in "the people" not as some vague and faceless mass, but as individual people with names and faces and life stories–each of which matter. If there ever genuinely was a place for such convictions on the Left, there is no more.

People of color, workers, the poor and gays are buying into their own ongoing enslavement and eventual destruction when they buy into the empty promises of the Left. It cannot really represent us because it will never lift us up. To retain power (which is what the Left really wants), it must hold us down. There's a reason "progressives" must continually remind us of all those hairy, scary bigots and tyrants on the Right. It's because in order to ensure their own political survival, they also need these trumped-up arch-villains to survive.

If we live in a statist society—one in which rival sides are always competing over which of their limited visions will control everyone by force—minorities of any kind will always remain vulnerable. But we are, actually, the canaries in the mine. *No* one dares to stay blissfully in the dark, because *everyone* is vulnerable. A group's power to enforce its will on anyone is, indeed, the power to force it on *anyone*.

Only on the Right are significant numbers of people even considering ending the game and bringing real power back to individual people. The Left has given up even imagining that as an option.

Is the Tea Party movement flawed? Of course it is. It is itself rent by two rival factions: one genuinely as libertarian as the movement's rhetoric implies and the other stealthily statist in unrelenting social reaction. In order for it to stay on course and true to its vision, the former must indeed decisively win the battle. But only the involvement of committed libertarians can help the Tea Party stay true to what it claims it wants to be.

The self-proclaimed progressives, who watch leftist prophets like Rachel Maddow on TV, read popular "progressive" blogs like the Daily Kos, and listen to whatever "Air America" is calling itself this week, weep and gnash their teeth over what's to become of real liberty in this country. Those among them who are serious in their concern, and not just blowing smoke, would do well to take a different course than making fun of the Tea Party. They are right that there are social reactionaries hiding within it, working—like termites in an outwardly-sound structure—to undermine it for their own purposes. But those of

140

us who truly do believe in liberty, instead of simply giving lip-service to it, should consider not beating the movement, but joining it. That is the best way (perhaps even the only way) to hold it on the course to which it has set itself.

Only those who really wish the cause of liberty to fail can content themselves with sitting on the sidelines and criticizing those who would protect our freedoms. If we don't choose to work within the Tea Party itself, we must still work in alliance with those who would be its better angels.

Leftists may aim to redistribute wealth, but they dare not permit the redistribution of power. That, they are bent on grabbing and keeping entirely for themselves.

The tradition of the modern Left has been one of socialist conformity. Its followers, for the most part kind and well-intentioned, have complacently allowed themselves to become little better than sheep. There appears to be nothing left of independence or freedom for those who back the powers-that-be on that side.

I look at two important indicators of the difference between Left and Right. It has been these indicators that have determined why I've left the Left and committed myself to the Right.

One indicator has been the very willingness of conservatives to embrace some libertarian ideals. When conservatives use the "L" word, some of them may do so cynically. They don't all really mean it (when their party's out of power, everybody tries to sound like a libertarian), but at least they aren't afraid to use the word.

On the Left, however, this particular "L" word is so deeply dreaded and loathed that it remains an epithet. A byword for all that's evil. They've gone from "speaking truth to power" under Bush 43 to toadying to Obama—though the latter, in many ways, has proven himself to be nothing more than Bush 44 with a Bolshevist vodka twist.

The twist, evidently, makes all the difference. And Marxism—

always the real goal of the Left—can *never* be reconciled with liberty.

As a lesbian, I know that particular "L" word has long been taboo on the political and religious Right. But the political Right and the religious Right—for all the latter's efforts—are by no means interchangeable. In the churches that welcome gays, many members remain politically conservative. H.L. Mencken once famously referred to the Episcopal Church (my own denomination) as "the Republican Party at prayer." This may no longer be by any means true, but there is still a healthy libertarian/economic conservative presence in the pews of this and many other mainline churches.

The fear and loathing I've encountered from leftists, because I'm a libertarian conservative, far exceeds any negative reaction I've gotten from most right-wingers because I'm gay. Only the most vehement social reactionaries still see all gays as evil. And they are no longer able to perpetuate lies about us, because other conservatives have gotten to know us as friends, relatives, coworkers, and neighbors. The lies only worked when, out of ignorance, most people didn't realize we were gay.

This brings me to the other indicator that the Right views libertarianism more hospitably than does the Left. Even if some do so cynically, social conservatives are embracing some libertarian ideals. They must now pretend to embrace them even if they'd rather not. On the Left, libertarianism—indeed, liberty itself—is the dreaded "L" word. Love of liberty is, for them, the love that dare not speak its name.

And regarding gays and lesbians, especially, the Left uses every dirty trick in their well-worn playbook. In the name of liberating us, they are intent on keeping us enslaved. We must be perpetually afraid, harassed, outraged, and oppressed. Though our "progressive" benefactors did nothing for us—even though they occupied the White House, enjoyed a huge majority in Congress, and were busily packing the courts—they continued to insist that they, and they alone, stood between us and certain doom at the hands of Right-Wing villainy.

The fact that one side still recognizes the importance of

individual liberty even enough to pay lip service to it, to wrap themselves in its mantle and to claim its principles for themselves, demonstrates that for one side—the Right—liberty and individual rights are not entirely dead. The Left has turned against these principles so completely that the very mention of them, the very concept of libertarianism, is now *verboten,* and liberty can be recognized as totally dead. There remains not even enough of the corpse for it, like the shells of Lenin or Brezhnev in the Kremlin, to be embalmed.

Are those on the Right always sincere in their belief that liberty matters? In the ongoing hold social reactionaries have on it, we can see that it is inconsistent. But there's a reason for the rule, in Tea Party-allied circles, that this particular "L" word remain in use. Among the real people in this country, a healthy love for liberty remains alive. Unlike the minions of "progressivism," they are yet a long way from becoming zombies who can be indoctrinated into doing whatever they are told.

Only on the libertarian Right can hope still be found for America's survival. It is the one source of hope I see. In this continued glimmer, I see a sign that my country may remain true to its founding principles and rise, from its statist stupor, to new vigor.

Those on the Right who are social reactionaries, hiding their actual dreams for a big-government takeover behind a libertarian façade, must maintain their pretense because most normal people view their real agenda with revulsion. Leftists don't understand why it is that, in the latter Bush years, the antics of the Right became so revolting. They don't realize that they were actually looking in a mirror. The Right loses elections when it strays from its founding principles. Absolutely nobody likes right-wingers when they behave like leftists—not even leftists.

There's a reason why horror movies and TV shows so often scare us with stories about zombies. Something deep inside of us recoils at the prospect of stumbling across the face of the earth as mere shells of our former selves—the undead, no longer truly alive. What

143

fascinates us, in these terrible stories, is that the undead still retain the resemblance of who they were when they were human. They wear the same clothes, tattered though they may be, and in their distorted expressions, before their noses fall off and their eyeballs roll out, we can still recognize nice old Uncle Harvey or sweet sister Sally. *Eeewww,"* we can't help thinking as they try to rip off the front door so they can bust in and eat our brains, *"I could end up just like that!*

I didn't want to be a zombie, so I left the Left. It is populated now, almost exclusively, by the undead. All the high-octane Marxist vodka in the world won't bring them to life again. They are very nice people—what's left of them. They really believe all the stuff they are being told. But nothing can make us rise again except for the real liberty, the true recognition of our humanity that makes us fully alive, and fully human.

On the Right, there yet remains hope not for zombie-fication, but for resurrection. I'll hold out for real humanity, and for an America fully alive.

Wil Losch
Public School Teacher; Rhinelander, WI

Wil Losch is a public school teacher who lives in Rhinelander, a small town in rural northern Wisconsin. Since 2004 he has been active in the development of charter schools, opening two of them for the School District of Rhinelander. He is a founding teacher of Northwoods Community Secondary School, a 6th to 12th grade project-based school where he still teaches today. He served as a curriculum writer and governing board member when the Rhinelander Environmental Stewardship Academy opened in 2007, serving middle school students in a place-based science academy. In 2010 he was awarded the prestigious Herb Kohl Teaching Fellowship, named after Wisconsin's long time Democratic senator. Losch built his family home in 2006, an energy efficient, solar powered, timber frame design made largely of local materials. In 2010 he was a Libertarian candidate for the 34th District of the State Assembly, receiving 10% of the vote, more than any other Libertarian candidate in the state that fall. Up until recent legislation in June 2011, state law required that he be a member of the Wisconsin Education Association Council (state teachers union) in order to teach in Wisconsin public schools.

Pencils, Pounding Nails, and Politics
My Libertarian Journey in Defense of Education and the Environment
by
Wil Losch

After Jerry Brown lost out to Bill Clinton in the 1992 presidential primaries, my interest and eventual vote went to Ross Perot. Looking back, this first presidential campaign in which I participated at the age of twenty would be a pretty solid predictor of my personal political evolution that followed. My heart and empathy was, and remains, with many causes of the Left, particularly support of strong schools and protection of natural resources. My undergraduate sociology and history professors either knowingly or unknowingly solidified my political launching point on the left side of our political spectrum when they taught me about social stratification, social inequality, class, and power in America.

Almost two decades later I have not abandoned my awareness of such concepts. Throughout the late 1990's and 2000's I've voted primarily for Democrats, occasionally intrigued by third-party candidates and independents. I've voted for Ralph Nader twice due to his concern for consumers, but I struggled to give him my vote over Al Gore in 2000 due to my hopes of Gore being more active in promoting governmental action regarding climate change. I've since learned (or remembered) that individual consumers can act on their own. John Kerry got my vote over Nader in 2004, because I didn't and still don't believe in illegal wars. I simply wanted G.W. Bush out. By 2008 I was a card carrying member of the Libertarian Party, but Barack Obama received my vote in the general election (Ron Paul received it in the primary). Obama's clear anti-war stance appealed to me.

As I approach the age of forty, the mid-point of most public sector careers, I've begun to reflect on my adult life as an education reformer, teacher and environmental advocate. I've concluded that modern day conservatives have been aided by modern day liberals in creating governments that hinder our schools and harm our

146

environment. The progressive champions I've supported haven't solved the problems. It was failure on my part to expect them too.

To help solve the problems I saw in education and with the environment, I began acting on my own, within my neighborhood schools and through building my own normal size, energy efficient home. This is when I learned that the Left is as adept as the Right in thwarting the actions of an individual. The understanding that individuals, not government programs, are the solutions to many of our collective challenges is what nurtured my interest in the liberty movement. It might also be why Democratic candidates are no longer guaranteed to receive a disproportionate amount of my votes in future years. In hopes of building the liberty movement, I vote for Libertarian candidates in all local and state elections when possible. Because the Libertarian platform is sensibly centrist, when voting in Federal elections I am drawn to candidates from either major party that play well with the other side and are not the first ones embraced by their respective, radical, liberty-crushing base.

School Reformer

Since 2004 my professional life has been that of a school reformer, doing my part to bring the free market characteristics of choice and competition to our public schools. During this time I concluded that teachers unions undermine the development of charter schools. And the Democratic Party all too often unthinkingly supports teacher's union opposition to charter schools. Learning these lessons was disheartening as I always believed that charter schools represent a choice for families and are also the experimental grounds where more creative, engaging, and relevant curricular models can be discovered for all schools to benefit from. Why wouldn't all teachers, union and political leaders support this?

The best example of my local teacher's union getting in the way of innovative charter school programming involved my wife, Nicole, who is also a teacher. When our youngest child was born Nicole took a year off, even knowing it could jeopardize her chances of working in the district again. After a full school year at home she was yearning to be out of the house a few hours a week. She met with local elementary charter school leaders about offering Spanish lessons to students in grades K-5. She spent late summer getting curriculum ready and was set to go when school started. Because of the greater flexibility of charter schools, the staff arranged a schedule that worked for my wife. Nicole worked five to seven hours a week for $17 per hour, a rate comparable to curriculum writing or tutoring pay in the district. Financial gain was not Nicole's main motivation, so she accepted this hourly wage that was below the per diem rate she earned as a full time teacher. But she was happy, school leaders were happy, the other charter teachers were happy, and Rhinelander had its first elementary foreign language program. It appeared to be a win-win-win-win situation! Spanish lessons started in September, the first week of school.

Then local union officials approached her about filing a grievance because she was not receiving her per diem rate based on a full time salary. We discouraged it and asked them not to do so. Nicole explained how it met her needs, how she was not being exploited, and how students were benefiting. A grievance was filed nonetheless. The Thursday morning before Halloween, the school principal confirmed to Nicole what she feared would come from this, telling her "The union has an issue with you teaching here. Clean your things out today." The short lived elementary foreign language program was finished. We later learned that an additional line of reasoning in shutting down our community's first ever elementary school foreign language program was that since every elementary student in the district could not receive lessons, then none should. Progressive? Hardly.

Defenders of the union would argue that the principle of not accepting lower wages is important. When considering the economic interests of the group, this is a fair argument. What was neglected through the union's action was a failure to recognize my wife's autonomy to act in a manner that fit both her needs and a flexible school's needs.   Furthermore, the local union's actions clearly demonstrated that perceived member benefits take priority over school improvement and student needs. It is important to know the true motivations of unions when they seek to advocate for school policy.

Unfortunately, teachers unions always say they are working for the benefit of the children. That clearly was not the case here. Teachers unions work for the economic interests of their group, even when that means ignoring the individual autonomy of one of their members or taking away opportunities for students.

Later, I further learned, during the 2008 elections, that the teacher's union/Democratic Party perspective does not always consider a charter school's legitimate concerns. After attending a local debate for our State Senate seat I approached both candidates during the informal visiting that followed. I had a specific point I wanted to share with both major party candidates. I spoke against a minor provision in proposed legislation that would affect teachers and schools in Wisconsin.

Wisconsin Education Association Council (WEAC) had lobbied for a provision that would place restrictions on teacher licensing, particularly the practice of teaching outside one's primary area of endorsement. Many charter schools operate as "one room school houses" where dynamic teachers are responsible for facilitating learning in many content areas, not just the area of their college major. The passing of such a provision would have instantly put many of Wisconsin's almost 200 charter schools in non-compliance. Surely, many would have simply closed. Traditional factory model schools where students are shuffled like cattle from room to room on bell schedules would be less impacted.

The Democratic candidate was short and wanted no long exchange. "It will probably die in committee" he said to placate me, suggesting that despite his support of the measure I shouldn't worry. The Republican candidate engaged me in a lengthy conversation, asking follow up questions about the consequences locally, and reiterating his belief that local decision making and "one size fits all" approach would not be supported by him. He earned my vote that night, becoming the first Republican I voted for in a general election. He earned it because, unlike the union supported Democrat, he was interested in what was best for keeping innovative public schools in operation. Once again, I was witnessing the effect of the teacher's union letting group economic interest work against the development of programs that benefit students, parents, and all our schools.

I have been accused of being anti-union. I'm actually not. I support voluntary association for the purpose of advocating group interests for any workers. But I do not support teacher's seeking group benefits at the expense of preventing change that benefits students. This is irresponsible and antithetical to the highest ideas of the profession. When teachers unions limit their advocacy of group economic interests to the period after decisions about the best programming have been made, then we will see teachers unions worthy of all our support and praise.

Home Builder

Next to education, a stronger record of protecting our environment caused me to support Democrats over Republicans in my early years. My environmental ethic drove me to build an energy efficient, small home—the opposite of the large McMansions being built around me. A small footprint, low electricity usage, and low ceilings would be key characteristics. Ground was broke in the summer of 2006. A three ring binder with the Wisconsin Uniform Building Code was always on site for two reasons. First, I assumed the code would assist me in building a safe, durable home. Second, being a law abiding citizen, I wanted to comply with all laws during this process. Little did I know that the latter would involve infringement of my personal choice on matters of taste in building design. The litany of codes in the Uniform Building Code made building my vision of a responsible home very difficult, actually impossible.

The residential building code dictates how many electrical outlets are in each room. "The code requires them" was a standard response from my electrician when questioned why certain walls or areas must have them. I'd guess that someone from the electricians' lobby helped this particular code get written. Hammering in more electrical boxes and the extra wiring required creates more work and income for electricians. Or perhaps it was someone from the realtor lobby. Maybe having homes with too few electrical outlets made selling homes more difficult. Maybe Home Depot and Lowes hired lobbyists. More electrical outlets create more opportunity to sell and plug in all sorts of appliances that they sell. I'm happy to see electricians work and stores move products, but not at the expense of my right to choose less.

I wanted to build our home so the entire south end of the structure was free from electrical wiring. I had two reasons for this. First, should I expand or remodel I knew I had one wall where I didn't need to worry about cutting or nailing into old wiring. Secondly, I didn't want my daily existence to be surrounded by electrical currents. Sounds odd and quirky? It is, but that is the beautiful thing about liberty, sometimes it is. As long as it does not infringe on another's rights what should it matter? In this case my liberty to be quirky, to build a home with fewer electrical outlets designed to support fewer electrical appliances was thwarted by government mandates.

Other headaches ensued after an inspector showed up at 5:00 am, only to leave an orange flag in the driveway with demeaning instructions to either proceed or call before proceeding. I never saw the inspector's face until the final home inspection where an "occupancy permit" would, hopefully, be granted. Today in Wisconsin and other states you can convince a bank to lend you tens of thousands of dollars and you can hire professionals to design and build the home, but you cannot take occupancy until the government says so. Since the inspector deemed that the house "looked lived in" the last thing he told me was that I forfeited a couple hundred dollars deposit—an imposition on my economic freedom to accompany the earlier hindrances of my personal choices.

Such a system of compliance could only be instituted by two mind sets. The first, as I speculated, from special interest lobbying. The second is a well intended desire to protect consumers, classifying consumers as potential victims that require pre-emptive care. This is an attitude too often embraced by the Left. Such an attitude ultimately says the government knows better than we do how our lives should be lived. So while the Right has also helped build such a system of freedom confining codes, I've seen no effort from the Left to dismantle them. Such codes prevented me building less of a house, a

151

more environmentally friendly house. This was not the most betraying action I'd experience from the Left.

Candidate

In 2010 I was a Wisconsin State Assembly candidate. Because I had the "gall" to run as a Libertarian, the Democratic Party and WEAC were not pleased. Local issues motivated and informed my campaign. A flawed public school funding formula that cheated taxpayers in my rural area was the primary issue I ran on. I ran a respectful campaign where I sought to be an open-book to all constituents. I talked and wrote at length on issues ranging from schools, tax breaks for select companies, building codes, or anything potential voters would ask me about. The one group I was not invited to speak with was WEAC. I was intentionally excluded from their candidate screening interviews. This did not stop WEAC from sending literature to its membership (including me) stating they surveyed and interviewed all the candidates. Such blatant lies were discouraging, especially coming from a group of which I was a member. "If you want to talk to us, run as a Democrat or Republican" was the snickering message I received from one of WEAC's state level political directors. Some local union officials advocated for my inclusion, but their requests fell upon the deaf ears of state union leaders. The words of the state director would not be the last radical statement I'd hear from union or party leaders.

The chair of one of the local county chapters of the Democratic Party called my place of employment questioning my ethics as a teacher, suggesting I was inappropriately distributing campaign materials to my students. Some of my students were very enthused about my campaign. The campaign itself was a heck of a project. I teach in a project-based school, so student questions and observations came up regularly. Most often they were not policy orientated questions, but process orientated. What exactly is a political party? How do you get your name on the ballot? Are debates required by law? Most students don't interact with candidates and campaigns, so when they found themselves this close to one, they asked questions. All student inquiries were handled with a professionalism that included sharing information when it was relevant to student content.

But I did separate my work as a campaigner from my work as a teacher. No students worked for or volunteered on my campaign.

Ironically, in two previous election cycles this same Democrat Party chair was a guest in my classroom, brought in for the sole purpose of sharing the Democrat platform with my students. As a teacher, I love election years. I invite party representatives and candidates from all levels of government into my classroom—to share their biases! I've had Republican, Democrat, Libertarian, Green, and Constitution Party candidates or leaders in my classroom over the last several election cycles.

After my campaign this same leader did little to halt the most extreme voices in his own party when I was threatened at a union/party meeting by a mentally unstable participant for "not being one of them." "He's drunk and probably not taking his meds." I was told. "I'm afraid of him too." Isn't the Left supposed to be the side that embraces peace and non-violence?

Ironically groups that the Left love to criticize for being close minded, such as right-wing Christian conservatives, treated me better during my campaign. One of the most rewarding nights of my campaign was being invited to speak to a Tea Party group called the "Northwoods Patriots." The Northwoods Patriots are a group of mostly staunch social conservatives that advocate for some fiscal conservative policies. I spent almost two hours speaking with them when they had twenty minutes slated for me on their agenda. I was comfortable when we discussed common issues such as zoning, building codes, local control, and the pitfalls for rural tourist areas of shared revenue tax systems. After an hour, I finally said "Look, I can talk to you all night about these things, but I'd be remiss if I didn't share with you the areas I feel we see things differently." Thus began another hour on social issues such as abortion and gay marriage. We spoke as neighbors seeking to understand the origins of each other's beliefs. Rather than boos and hisses, I received affirming head nods and there were times I got hearty laughter from the crowd.

One member, who adamantly opposed gay marriage, said "Isn't it the role of the state to promote a growing citizenry? If the state promotes gay marriage that is threatened."

"Sir, based on my work with teenagers, I don't think we are ever in danger of not replenishing the state's citizenry. They are ready to go." I replied with non sharp-tongued intent. Even he shook his head and laughed with the others at the realization of the fallacy of his logic. I concluded by suggesting the state has no role in any marriage, that all arrangements are merely contracts between adults and any two seeking to enter such a contract should be allowed to do so. Let individual churches, as private organizations, define marriage. I found myself not nearly as polarized with this group, and here I was tackling head-on some of the most divisive wedge issues of our age. If only WEAC members had such manners as these right-wingers.

Conclusion

I've always viewed Republicans as the group that undercuts public education by the over promotion of cookie cutter curriculums, standards, and standardized tests. How can creative, customized classrooms exist with such a paradigm driving policy? Furthermore, isn't the absence of, or discouragement of, local control contradictory to conservative values? So I quickly began to view Republican rhetoric as hypocritical. But starting charter schools brought me up against the lobbying forces of teachers unions and the candidates they support, largely Democrats. The Left's efforts to standardize the school environment, for the well intended purpose of protecting workers, has played an equal role in hindering creative, customized classrooms.

I've also always viewed Republicans as the group that opens up the door for the over exploitation and destruction of natural resources. Usually this is justified with free market rhetoric, but the truth is, the policy that followed rarely promoted free markets. Rather, the status quo was supported in the energy sector and innovation seems slow. Reliance on fossil fuels grows, CO_2 keeps getting pumped into the atmosphere at historic levels before we even fully understand the consequences, and I'm ending my thirties as they began, with my country heavily engaged in war in the Middle East. A subtly dangerous byproduct of all this is that free market rhetoric becomes unfairly associated with environmental degradation. Through all this, I viewed Republican lawmakers as failing to grasp the most basic of economic principles: the long term health of our environment and our economy are inextricably linked, as one goes, so goes the other.

These days I find myself politically homeless on the traditional linear spectrum and pretty discouraged by the two major parties in our country. Libertarians certainly speak to my experience and views today. As an educator I often remind my students that ending an inquiry with more questions is acceptable as long as those questions are the result of new thinking taking place.

How do teachers unions hinder the much needed reform our schools and students need to compete and live in a globalized world that faces many economic and environmental challenges? Why does the government need to regulate superficial details of how our homes are designed? Isn't it enough if my banker, builder, architect, and I all feel good about the project? Are building codes and zoning laws more about defining our neighbors' space over our own? Why don't teachers unions see their lobbying and candidate endorsement process as equally harming to democracy and biased as right leaning groups? Have organizations on the Left become as much, or more, close minded as groups on the Right?

Groups on the Left show unwillingness to grapple with such questions. As stated previously, my heart lies with many issues dear to the Left. I also value personal autonomy. When the Left integrates this with causes such as public education or protection of natural resources, the Left will have my support again. Not until then.

Ron T. Mahnert
College Student; Putnam Valley, NY

My name is Ron T. Mahnert. I am a 21 year old white male. I was born, raised, and still live in Putnam County, New York. Currently I am a senior psychology major at Stony Brook University also located in New York State. When not at school I work installing duct work for heating and cooling systems. My hobbies include interest in libertarianism (of course), free market principles, and philosophical and psychological aspects of politics, as well as reading, writing, hiking, photography, and hypnotism.

College Sophomore Strays from the Left
by
Ron T. Mahnert

Politics was a field I seldom involved myself in intellectually prior to my sophomore year of college. I held political beliefs for most of my life, but never put much effort into explaining why I held these views. At that time in my life I identified as a liberal. I had a few minor reasons for taking this stance, mainly influences from having family and friends that were to the left side of the political spectrum. The main reason for my former beliefs, however, was I believed that government was the answer to all problems. Around the end to the second decade of my life I began seeing government's role differently and entered a political metamorphosis.

On Election Day November 4, 2008 I remember being ecstatic over the Barack Obama victory. Finally the White House would have a Democrat in the executive branch after the downward slope of the George W. Bush era. I thought we would see the end of the wars in Afghanistan and Iraq and the abolishment of the Patriot Act. At that time I was also excited for the expansion of government control over health care. After all, government would be able to deal with any corruption in the United States health system and deliver better services to the poor. The free market was too corrupt with big business to help in a way similar to that.

Almost a year passed since the election and I was still content with the results. Honestly, I had no idea what Obama had been doing to improve the country as I only spent minute attention on White House affairs. Nevertheless, America had a liberal president, thus I knew he was doing an excellent job at bringing the country towards the right direction.

It was around this time that my change toward libertarian ideals began. The midpoint of the first semester of my college sophomore year was approaching; there would shortly be many midterms and much stress. One night in an effort to relieve that stress I decided to watch some random online videos. A friend showed me a website a few years back about a conspiracy that stated all the world's most powerful and influential people were not actually people, but a group of aliens. I had watched some crazy videos of this genre before and I decided to watch some more on that night. They were always worth a good laugh. The conspiracy videos I found, however, differed from those extraterrestrial ones. They discussed how there is no hope or change as Obama, Bush, and many of the previous presidents worked together toward one goal of eroding American citizens of their rights and money to provide the government with more power.

Immediately I rejected these ideas. Despite this initial rejection, however, I continued watching more of these videos over the next few nights. A couple caught my eye as they mentioned that Obama not only will not conclude the wars, but will expand America's military actions. I thought to myself that it was true Obama did not end either the war in Iraq or Afghanistan yet, but he had been busy with other things (still not knowing what those "things" were). A few days later I had read that Obama was planning to expand the war effort in Afghanistan. I could not believe that those crazy conspiracy theories had been correct about this event. My trust in government declined, whether Republicans or Democrats held a majority of the power.

Although my trust descended in government, I also quickly gave up what little faith I had in conspiracy theories. They were too pessimistic as well as contradictory. The videos left any viewer feeling helpless, as if it were fate that big government will win in the end no matter what action was taken by the people. I also had trouble imagining that all politicians were innately evil and planned for world domination. Then the few solutions offered contradicted the message of the videos. A majority claimed that both government and big business worked together to eliminate people's rights. The solution to this problem was more government involvement in the market. I did manage to leave the conspiracy culture with two important insights: do not always trust those holding authority positions and, despite its intentions, government has gained too much power.

During my short lived conspiracy phase, I read an important piece of literature on major disasters in history. It started out as a required book needed for a sociology class, but has influenced me more than most any other. The book, *A Paradise Built in Hell* by Rebecca Solnit, described how both people and government reacted in times of crisis. Through Solnit's examples of the 1906 San Francisco Earthquake, 9/11, Hurricane Katrina, and others, it is easy to pick out a common theme found between them: when government gets involved, the disaster escalates. Usually people are resourceful and team up to deal with the crisis. The idea that there is mass panic and chaos among individuals and that government is necessary to solve these problems is debunked by Solnit. Solnit's book became a primary source in altering my belief in government as the solution to problems, to government as the cause of problems.

The semester was coming to a close at that point. If my faith in Obama had been a flame when he was elected, it now resembled an ember. Further events, such as Climategate, led me to distrust liberals even more. Government involved environmental protection used to be one of the main issues I looked for in a political candidate. Climategate made me realize that there could not only be fraud in the supposed scientific data, but also that different scientists yielded different results as to when or if climate change will have its most severe effects. The belief that climate change is a manmade disaster is also questionable. In my opinion, for government, a non-scientific organization, to dictate how we should live our lives dependent upon the research they receive from one scientist while ignoring another does not provide a good solution to environmental problems.

When the semester ended I no longer saw myself as a liberal. Politically I did not know what to consider myself. I had yet to learn what a libertarian is. In *A Paradise Built in Hell* they mentioned libertarians, but I grouped them together with anarchists and did not see that as the best way to describe myself. For a while I walked alone in political isolation.

Then I discovered a particular Congressman from Texas, Ron Paul. I learned about his positions and saw his voting record. I would think, "A Republican that voted against military funding and the Patriot Act? There are liberals who have not done that. Who is this guy?" I further learned that he considered himself one of these libertarian guys. I know now that he is not the perfect libertarian and that I disagree with him on some issues, but he is the congressman I most identify with politically.

It was soon after discovering Paul that I went on to research the Libertarian Party. While reading the Party's platform I realized it was exactly where I fit into the political spectrum. Prior to this point I had mostly seen my leave from the Left as caused by frustration from what was not being accomplished and broken political promises. I came to believe, though, that libertarians hold a more sophisticated intellectual argument for their positions than do liberals. My beliefs had not only evolved politically, but philosophically as well. I began to see people as mostly good and willing to help one another as opposed to my old thinking that people were only looking out for themselves with required government intervention to make people do good deeds. I changed from a disgruntled individual brought down by the political norm, to an optimist believing a new path could be paved.

Today I look back at my leave from the Left without any regrets. It was a lonely voyage from the start. After discovering others hold similar beliefs, I have come to feel more at home with my position. Now I feel I have a better sense of community with libertarians than I had with the Left.

Robert P. Marcus
Entrepreneur and Chief Executive Officer
of RGB Spectrum; Alameda, CA

Bob Marcus has 44 years of diversified business experience, with a track record in entrepreneurship, general management, marketing, and finance. Bob is currently CEO of RGB Spectrum, a company he founded, which manufactures advanced AV and IT equipment. The company serves customers in military, security, early responder, and medical markets worldwide. RGB is a $40+ million company experiencing rapid growth.

As co-founder and CEO of Abel Image Research, Bob recruited the management team, positioned an advanced 3-D graphics product for CAD/CAM and simulation, and consummated the first major sales into aerospace and other industries.

As a consultant to Robert Abel and Associates, a special effects video production company, Bob restructured the company financially and organizationally, setting the stage for rapid growth from $6 million to $20 million within three years.

As VP-Pacific of ICS Interway, Bob had line responsibility for operations in the Far East and US West Coast for this international transportation company. He doubled the size of his division in two and a half years to over $10 million.

Bob has a strong international business background, including career positions in Hong Kong, Singapore, and Indonesia. He is also the holder of several patents and patents pending, most recently in UAV technology. Bob received his MSIM in 1966 from the Sloan School, Massachusetts Institute of Technology.

I Was a Teenage Liberal
by
Robert P. Marcus

Any man who is under thirty, and is not a liberal, has not heart; and any man who is over thirty, who is not a conservative, has no brains.

Winston Churchill

I admit it. Back in the '60s I went to Columbia University and emerged as a modern liberal. I had a belief in government by the best and brightest, though my politics were otherwise somewhat vague.

In the cloistered halls of my college, I didn't meet many non-liberals. I assumed they were mainly denizens of totalitarian states and Third World sinkholes, plus a few misbegotten souls somewhere in the Deep South. Later, when I actually spent time in the South, I met people who styled themselves conservatives and who were, surprisingly to me, both compassionate and intelligent. This presented something of a conundrum, given my view that only modern liberals so qualified. I solved it by deciding that these people were really liberals; they just didn't like the word. How's that for logic—when confronted with facts that challenged my beliefs, I simply changed the facts. Liberal dogma stayed intact. As I was later to learn, I was not alone in my conceit *cum* political philosophy.

The term "liberal" does have *caché*. I sometimes discover people who are not really modern liberals in any ideological sense of the word, but who are enamored of the label and refuse to see themselves differently. The very idea of doing so engenders a bad reaction, like waking up in a Kafkaesque nightmare to discover you are a giant cockroach.

Modern liberals derive their political philosophy not from classical liberalism but from late-nineteenth-century progressivism. Nevertheless, while vague on the provenance of their ideology they are supremely confident of their compassion and intelligence, and eager to force their political vision on those who do not share their mental and moral advantages. I discovered that liberalism is less a political philosophy than a state of mind.

Ask modern liberals, "What is the purpose of government?" Almost invariably they think it's a trick question. When pressed, their answer is usually some variation on "To make people healthy, wealthy, and wise." Fair enough, but that is not what the founders of our country had in mind. As stated in the Declaration of Independence, governments are instituted to preserve our rights. That is the purpose of government, no more and no less.

Liberals read the Declaration without realizing how far we have strayed from its precepts. It's almost as if they visualized a different Declaration, a Declaration of the Divine Right of Liberals:

> "We hold these Truths to be self-evident, that some Men are created more compassionate and intelligent than others, that they are endowed by their Creator with certain unalienable Rights, that among these are Welfare, Redistribution, and the Pursuit of Cosmic Justice. That to manifest their Paternalism, Governments are instituted among Men, basing their populism on the Politics of Envy; that whenever any Rule of Law becomes destructive of these Ends, it is the Right of Liberals to reinterpret it, and to institute new meaning, laying its Foundation on such Prejudices, and in such Form, as to them shall seem most likely to effect their Will over others."

Winston Churchill famously suggested that liberalism is an affliction of the young and idealistic, an affliction that in a healthy individual runs its course with age. For me, recovery started in my twenties, though it took some time.

I was still in college when JFK issued his famous dictum, "Ask not what your country can do for you; ask what you can do for your country." Now, I was OK with the first clause; I had a long wish list for my family, friends, and especially for my girlfriend, but little that I actually wanted from my government other than to keep the streets safe. Okay, maybe subsidized student loans, but that was about it.

164

On the other hand, what was I supposed to do for my country, except to pay taxes on my small earnings and stand ready to put on a uniform when my student deferment was up? I thought of signing up for NROTC (the Navy version of ROTC), but I couldn't qualify because of my uncorrected vision. That seemed idiotic to me, since there would be plenty of room for my eyeglasses on a battleship, and even on smaller vessels.

After I graduated I took an interest in the Foreign Service. I went through an inept screening process and met some very mediocre people. Doubts began to creep in. The final straw was a pamphlet entitled "Protocols for a Junior Foreign Service Officer." The chapter on seating people at a table expounded the various rules, but for groups of a certain size it was impossible to meet them. It was suggested that one simply not have groups of those unfortunate sizes. What was one to do—not invite someone who should have been invited, or invite someone who shouldn't have been? I decided that perhaps this was not an organization in which I would prosper. I finally despaired of any job in the public sector. Noble as government service might be, I could best serve my country by being a good citizen, paying my taxes, and adding to the gross national product.

I learned a lot about liberalism over the years, sometimes in surprising circumstances. I attended a private showing of a film called *Prejudice*, which was supposed to be a study of racial discrimination. It centered on a group of men of various races discussing how they were either the perpetrators (the whites) or the victims (everyone else) of prejudice. No one fitted into a neutral category. Just perpetrators and victims. The group made short work of one man who steadfastly held that he was neither. I remember one black guy complaining about how uncomfortable he felt walking through a certain community. Prejudice? It just so happened that a few weeks earlier I found myself driving in that same forbidding place. I locked my car doors, hunkered down in my seat, and fingered my can of Mace. And I'm not black. Some neighborhoods are just not that friendly.

The discussion period after the documentary was what I would label "a liberal guilt wallow." Virtually every attendee was beating his breast and confessing personal responsibility for racism, even slavery.

A number of white haired women who looked like Norwegian grandmothers confessed to all kinds of guilt, though always nonspecifically. When it was my turn—we were all expected to confess—I started by pointing out, no insult intended, that the overwhelming majority of the people there came from good peasant stock, like myself. I stated categorically that I owned no slaves and neither had my father, though we had not discussed the matter. But I'm sure he would have mentioned it if he had.

I tried to make clear that I was not insensitive to issues of prejudice, having, as a Jew, been on the receiving end of both subtle and unsubtle forms of it. Nevertheless, not all the problems in life are attributable to prejudice. The fault, dear Brutus, lies in ourselves sometimes. I pointed out that I had black friends, and that my fraternity in college was the first to pledge blacks. I was pledge master at the time, and I might add that I scrupulously saw that they had to swallow exactly the same number of goldfish that everyone else did. *Disclaimer: No goldfish were harmed in this event.* No matter; afterward I was surrounded by a circle of silence and treated like an unrepentant sinner at a revival meeting.

So what is modern liberalism? It has a murky history and a dark side—a willingness to force solutions on people who do not want them. A dictionary definition of modern liberalism might read as follows:

Modern liberalism . . . the heartfelt desire to impose one's values and choices on the powerless for their own good (cf. conservatism, which also sanctions coercion, but heartlessly);

in politics . . . the belief that all human problems can be solved by wise government and tax dollars;

in philosophy . . . the Platonic ideal of a government of the best and brightest, without a clue about how to achieve it;

in economics . . . the belief that free markets are suspect and that capitalism is inherently immoral (cf. Marxism-lite);

in psychology . . . the self-congratulatory delusion that one holds a monopoly on compassion and intelligence;

in race relations . . . a modern belief in "the white man's burden";

in law . . . a belief that the constitution is a mere collection of words, given meaning only by current political appointees, based on their social-political prejudices and without reference to original meaning or intent (cf. Newspeak);

in morality . . . a belief that good intentions are more important than consequences;

in government . . . a belief that any government program is workable, given good intent and more funding;

in theology . . . the New Age belief that we can heal the world through wallowing in guilt;

in public policy . . . a curious belief that consenting adults should be free of government interference in the bedroom but not in the workplace.

For a depiction of the darker side of modern liberalism, there is none better than *Rabbit Proof Fence*, a movie about Australian aborigines who were taken from their families to give them the putative advantages of white culture, and through selective breeding, white color. That was 1960s Aussie liberalism. The roads to hell are usually paved with good intentions. An inquisitor crams something down your throat (or up the other end) to save your soul; a conservative does it for the good of society; a liberal does it for your own good.

Fortunately, as Churchill hoped would happen to all young people, my infatuation with liberalism ran its course. The decline began with a question I posed to myself while still in college: If legislators are so smart, how do we get such bad laws? I couldn't come up with an answer.

Admittedly, it was a complex question. The answer awaited my reading of Henry Hazlitt's treatise on concentrated benefits and distributed costs, *Economics in One Lesson*, many years later. But that question was the first chink in my liberal belief in the concept of government by the best and brightest.

I had another *aha!* moment when I spent three months in the South on a training assignment. I shared an office with a John Bircher. On one hand, he had the most distorted worldview of anyone I had ever met. On the other hand, he was intelligent and willing to engage in discussions without rancor. I found that he had a consistent (if sometimes odious) belief system, he spoke with candor, and he possessed a lively wit and sense of humor. He referred to the then new base metal coinage that had entered circulation under President Johnson as "LBJ slugs." Imagine that—a sense of humor on an ultraconservative! Of course, the only thing really surprising was my surprise, but such was my own inexperience and prejudice.

I met a lot of other conservatives during that sojourn, people whose worldviews were very similar to my own, without the belief in the advantages of government by the best and brightest—decent, hardworking, educated people. It became clear that conservatives were more a more varied and complex lot than I had imagined.

Then I discovered the Cato Institute. From there it was all downhill: Ayn Rand, Milton Friedman, Thomas Sowell, F.A. Hayek. Funny how none was included in my prescribed readings in college. I checked. There was a bit of Adam Smith, but only a small fraction of the pages devoted to Karl Marx. Really; I counted the pages. There was also some Locke and Hume and other classical liberals, who bore a similar name through no resemblance to modern liberals.

It was with the classical liberals that I eventually found my belief system: the sovereignty of the individual, self-ownership, individual responsibility, free association, voluntary exchange, free markets, limited government, inalienable rights, the rule of law. Heady stuff. A set of concepts worth living by and fighting for.

I can go to a liberal guilt wallow with impunity—if anyone asks me back.

Caroline C. Meckel
Law School Student; Vernon, CT

Caroline Carpenter Meckel, daughter of Dan and Molly Carpenter, was born in Hartford, CT and lived in Stamford, CT until age ten, when her family moved to Simsbury, CT. She currently lives in Vernon, CT with her husband, Steven Meckel. For high school she attended Suffield Academy (Class of 2004). She matriculated at Trinity College (Class of 2008) where she majored in English Literature and double minored in Philosophy and Women, Gender, and Sexuality Studies. She is currently a student at Qunnipiac University School of Law, projected to graduate in 2014.

Her future plans are narrowly limited to graduating from law school and continuing to play rugby for the Hartford Wild Roses. In addition to rugby, reading, writing and her husband, Caroline loves dogs and still enjoys working with children after her volunteer teaching experiences in Hartford, CT. Her current ambition is to either become a best-selling author or a Supreme Court Justice. But, today is Tuesday. On Fridays, her ambition is usually only to live on the beach in Rhode Island selling hemp necklaces for beer money and doing absolutely nothing besides.

Old Enough to Know Better, Still Young Enough to Care
by
Caroline C. Meckel

When I was in college, my dad used to tease me with his version of the famous Winston Churchill quote: "If you're not liberal when you're young, you have no heart. If you're not conservative when you're old, you have no head."[1] My mother used to (and still does) call me her "little free radical".[2] In college, I identified as a liberal Democrat. My political realignment to libertarian was based not on a change of heart, but rather, a change of mind about the role and scope of government. It has been an evolution of my personal philosophy based on post-college experiences working in the real world.

My political "coming of age" occurred somewhere between graduating from high school and entering college during the 2004 election. My identification as a liberal was based on a strong belief in the rights of the individual balanced with the idea that, as a society, those who have more should empathize with those who have less, and do what they can to help—especially when it comes to the basic necessities of life. To me, in 2004 (and in 2008), the Democrats represented the party that championed women's rights, supported equality in diversity in lifestyle and culture, and the people who were working hard to close the economic gap between the rich and the poor. While the Republicans claimed to be the party that supports the right of the individual against government intrusion, the party's focus on denying women the full spectrum of reproductive choices, denying the gay community the right to marry, and their insistence that Christian morals are the only kind of morals seemed like the worst kind of hypocrisy. I was turned off—even though, fiscally and socially, I believed the less government the better (a value I inherited from my parents).

My parents are Republicans and have been so their whole lives. My mother was field director for the state of Connecticut for George H. W. Bush's 1980 campaign and worked for the Republican National Committee until 1986, when I was born. My father is a tax attorney/entrepreneur whose entire career has been dedicated to advocating restraint on government power, especially in the form of taxation.

I think my greatest political achievement to date was not the work I put in volunteering for a local Democratic mayoral campaign—it was convincing both of my parents to vote for the Democratic candidate in the 2004 and 2008 presidential elections. Both of them, as am I, were disgusted with the Right's focus on limiting the civil rights of individuals with whose lifestyles they disagree and contradictory actions—an example of the latter is calling for less government, while simultaneously giving the government more power to intrude on the lives of its citizens with legislation like the Patriot Act.

My mother (who used to despise the Clintons) went with me to see Hillary speak when she came to Hartford. She was beginning to feel like the Republican Party was letting her down, (especially when McCain chose Palin for a running mate). She felt, as I do, that the Republican Party has been hijacked by religious zealots and the kind of nationalistic patriotic fervor that leads to innocent blood being shed.

I inherited from my parents not only my sense of values respecting individuals' rights to be individuals, but also an interest in community service. While we lived in Stamford, Connecticut both of my parents volunteered often. My mother tutored children with special needs at my elementary school. My father coached soccer. He coached not only my team, but also created a program that allowed children from poorer families to play for free. He provided them with t-shirts for uniforms and sometimes equipment when necessary. When we moved to Simsbury, Connecticut my parents became very active in organizing the town soccer club and my father continued to coach youth soccer.

I attended Trinity College—a quasi-conservative liberal arts bubble in the middle of urban, inner city Hartford (an otherwise promising city strangled by poverty, gangs, and drug violence). While there I majored in English Literature and double minored in Philosophy and Women, Gender, and Sexuality Studies. Through my studies and my social life (I belonged to Zeta Omega Eta, the first, and to my knowledge the only, feminist sorority in the US; I also played—

and continue to play—women's rugby) I became increasingly interested and involved in social issues. I did considerable community service through Zeta—including helping organize and run youth seminars for middle school girls in Hartford, raising money for local women's shelters and other charities, and participating yearly in Do-It-Day, Trinity's only community service focused day.

With all the fire and righteous indignation that only a liberal arts education can induce in a young woman, I went into the post-college world believing I could change it through idealism and energy alone. I was excited to begin my AmeriCorps-sponsored teaching job at a brand new private middle school for boys. I was especially excited to finally have the chance to actually "do" rather than just theorize. I was convinced that I would change lives, inspire my students to greatness, and somehow find the answer to solving all the problems with education in our country—and in so doing, help to end the cycle of poverty and violence which has been so detrimental to urban youth.

Disillusionment, I've found, is the adult version of freshman orientation.

My year of AmeriCorps teaching was one of the most amazing experiences of my life. Detailing my experiences there deserves a small novel; but suffice to say, it changed me and changed my mind about the way I viewed politics and the role and scope of government involvement in the welfare of our citizens.

I entered The School a bleeding heart liberal, ready to verbally skewer anyone who argued that the government should not be using our tax dollars to provide a safety net for the most disadvantaged and vulnerable members of society[3]. My general attitude was such that I believed that no child we taught could not be "saved" (i.e. brought up to grade level, taught the importance of an education, and put on a path to a successful life) if I cared enough, sacrificed enough, and really gave it everything I had.

It is a cruel trick of memory that we remember our defeats so much more clearly than our successes. While I have many good memories of my teaching experiences and I know that I did a great deal of good for my students—it is the negative experiences that seared into my memory. Ultimately, the positive experiences shaped my political thought, but the negatives forced the change.

The School's mission is to provide a safe and structured learning environment for bright and hardworking students who wish to use education as a vehicle for upward mobility. The goal is to prepare each student so they can be accepted by private high schools, receive the very best high school education, and thus be motivated to pursue higher education as well. The School was founded on a Jesuit model in New York City. The School is funded and run entirely through private donations, grants, and volunteerism. Discipline and hard work are the core values of The School. And it is not just the students who are expected to work hard—but also the parents and the teachers/volunteers. The School functions on the idea that there is an agreement between the children and the adults that all of us will work as hard as we can to help the students succeed.

The hours are grueling for both the students and teachers. Most of the students were used to receiving little or no homework in public school and most could not afford to participate in after school activities. They receive at least two hours of homework a night, are required to participate in after school sports, and if their grades are not up to par, are also required to return to school after dinner to participate in evening study.[4] Teachers are expected to teach, coach, and supervise evening study, and be available on Saturdays for athletic events and field trips. Most of us average 80 hours of work time in a week (in exchange for room, board, minimal health insurance, and a living stipend of $300 a month). The parents also have duties to perform. They have to provide transportation for their sons to and from school (including picking them up at 5:00 after sports and returning them at 6:30 for evening study).

There are no lunch or meal services, so the parents have to provide lunch for their sons (most of our kids were on the free meal programs in public schools). Parents are also required, once a month, to bring in a home cooked meal for lunch for the teachers. And, of course, they are expected to support their sons as best they can by helping with homework and staying in communication with teachers.

My most disillusioning moments involved the expulsion of students who were beyond our ability to help. The expulsion of one boy, (we'll call him Casey) in particular, I took especially to heart because I blamed myself for it. I still have a picture of him playing chess with my husband (then boyfriend) while we waited for his mother to pick him up after evening study; she was almost always late, both to pick him up and drop him off. He was very bright and had a lot of academic potential. At times, he could be sweet and loving and funny. But, most of the time, he was very angry. As nice as he could be at times—he was a bully. A combination of too many detentions (lateness, undone homework, disruptiveness in class), and too many complaints from other parents about his bullying ensured that the boy was on thin ice. It didn't help that his mother was constantly late to drop him off and pick him up.[5] She missed parent-teacher meetings. She often "forgot" to pack him a lunch (he used to compliment me on my peanut butter and jelly sandwiches; he liked that I always remembered to cut the crust off and slice them diagonally). I recall her bringing us lunch once in the few months he was a student. The last straw was a rather nasty incident when he and a classmate decided to destroy the fifth grade class projects. It was on my watch that the projects were destroyed.

I agonized for a long time about him. He troubled me more than the others who left. There was the boy's accomplice in crime, who liked to pretend he was a tornado in the classroom when he thought no one was looking. We couldn't re-use any of his books after he'd left; they were graffittied and torn. I witnessed him tear the coat rack off the wall just for the fun of it. His grandmother yelled and cursed at me so loudly during parent-teacher conferences after she saw my comment that he might have some anger issues that the principal had to intervene on my behalf.

There was the boy who wrote "F--- Ms. - " (now the principal of the school, years later) and refused to confess even when the entire school was made to stand in line during recess until someone stepped forward. His eventual breakdown into tears gave him away, though he still denied doing it. He was eventually expelled for physically attacking another student. I felt sorry for his aunt who pleaded for us to keep him; she was an extremely nice woman with her hands very full. She was taking care of both him and his mother.

Others left voluntarily; they couldn't handle the academics or their parents couldn't handle the transportation schedule. We pleaded with one woman who was planning on having her son go back to the public school at the end of the year. He was one of my sixth grade Math students, an extremely bright and kind boy, though it was like pulling teeth to get him to do his homework. He, too, was constantly late, though was always upset about it and embarrassed when his mother forgot her duties. I remember how he went out of his way to help other students who struggled, though he was often uninterested in his own work. His mother just didn't seem to understand. She cared more about the fact that it would be easier for her if he could just take the bus.

There were three different boys with learning disabilities who left. One had a severe memory/retention problem. At 14 he was still in the sixth grade and could barely read, write or do any basic work with numbers. I had him for Math. During one test, he just gave up and cried on his desk. I remember, he asked me why he was stupid. One of the volunteers, a nun, pulled some strings to get him into a school for kids with severe learning problems and found a sponsor who was willing to pay his tuition. The boy's mother refused to accept that her son had any problems and blamed us for his failing grades.

I still agonize the most over Casey, though. His mother's final words still haunt me as she pulled him, sobbing, out the door. I was very upset when he was expelled. I blamed myself for allowing him to leave the room during detention to go sharpen his pencil, giving him the opportunity to damage the projects. I was outside the principal's office, making copies of the math exam I was to administer that afternoon when they left. I was trying very hard not to cry when I heard him start crying and pleading to stay. On the way out, she noticed me and stopped. I had my head down fighting to keep back the tears that kept threatening to come. I wanted so very badly to go console the boy—to give him some sort of advice, some sort of comfort. But, I knew I should not. I hoped by maintaining a stony indifference he would finally understand that negative actions bring negative consequences—and his punishment was not just expulsion from a school, but expulsion from a safe place where people cared about him and wanted him to succeed.

The mother stopped and pointed at me. "See, no one here cares about you. No one's going to help you. Nobody cares. You're on your own."

The principal, mercifully, left me leave early that day. I spent most of my afternoon driving around the city aimlessly observing the unintelligible lines that divided the nice neighborhoods from the rough ones—the children playing in the streets, their only apparent adult supervision were the shady men on the corners, whom, in my bitterness and depressed mood, I assumed were drug dealers and thugs, waiting only for the kids to be old enough to recruit for their gangs. I ended up in the parking lot of a Burger King, and not knowing what else to do I called my mother and told her everything that had happened.

Through my sobbing incoherence she managed to piece together the story. She shared with me similar experiences she had while tutoring in Stamford, admitting that some of those experiences contributed greatly for our move to suburban Simsbury. I won't ever forget what she told me that day: "Honey, you can't save them all. Focus on the ones you can help, steel yourself against the ones you can't. You have to save a little of you for yourself."

I will always be grateful for the support my parents and (now) husband gave me through that year—but I am even more grateful for the (mutual) support of my fellow teachers, volunteers, and especially from Eddie. Eddie was the night shift guard at the front desk of the YWCA that houses The School. He was part counselor and mentor to all of the teachers. I think, without him, most of us would have gone insane. We all had our heart to hearts with Eddie upon leaving on bad days.

Eddie worked in one of the public schools during the day. He helped us put things in perspective. We were a small school where the majority of the students were good kids with good families who wanted to succeed. Our own mini-dramas and tragedies were nothing compared to what he witnessed daily at his school. His message was even harsher than my mother's, "Girl, you can't save them all; you'll kill yourself trying". He told us stories about the girls and boys he tried to mentor—his own personal failures and successes. My own heartbreak over the boys who left or were forced to leave seemed trivial when Eddie told me about a pregnant 14-year old who dropped out of school or a 15-year old boy being shot in a gang-related incident. He shrugged off the failures: there were always more kids who needed help, and he didn't have time to waste on the ones who resisted it.

Eddie and my mother were not the only ones to give me the message. I started playing rugby again that spring. Several of my teammates worked in public schools—most in the city, some in the suburbs. Each of them had taken Eddie's and my mother's advice to heart. And they certainly were not bad people. They cared very much about their students—but they were (and still are) realistic about which students they can or cannot reach and set aside plenty of time for themselves so that they can have the emotional strength and energy to do their jobs.

That message went against every instinct, moral, and goal I had when I decided I wanted to teach. The failures I experienced there were a cold splash of reality that dampened my liberal fire. But rather than extinguishing it, that passion I entered with hardened, like hot steel doused in water.

In conversations with parents, I realized that one of the great successes of The School is that it *is* helping its students have a chance to break the cycle of poverty in which they are all caught. The School started in 2008 (I was in the original class of teachers). We started with just a 5th and 6th grade. In the spring of 2011, those left of the original 6th graders have all graduated, and each of them is attending a prestigious private high school this coming fall. The remaining 5th grade class is graduating in the spring of 2012, with the same terrific result.

Why does this school succeed when a many public schools fail? I think there are several good answers to this question, but the most pertinent to my political re-alignment has to do with the kind of services The School offers its students, the parents accepting the responsibilities we requested, and the students meeting the academic and behavioral expectations of the school.

For example, the majority of our students qualified for free meal programs at the public schools. We as I mentioned, does not provide this. The parents manage to get their kids fed (and feed the teachers once a month, too). I am not advocating that any child should ever go hungry, but I am suggesting that where there is a will, there is a way. If the service is not provided, the parents will find a way (or, like we did for Casey, the teachers will).

A big reason why public schools are failing to provide an adequate education for its students is due to a failure of the teachers to manage the classrooms. Classroom management was one of the biggest struggles in the first year teaching. I only had 15 students in my Reading/Language Arts class and I struggled to teach for the first few weeks. Even the high achieving students had difficulty with authority and seemed not to know proper classroom etiquette (raising hands, respecting the teacher, being quiet while others are speaking, not fidgeting or moving, concentrating on the lesson, etc.). By the end of the year, I had 11 students and still struggled at times. Even just one child who becomes a disruption can throw off the whole class (a child like Casey for-example). Imagine a class of 30 plus, half with learning disabilities or emotional/behavioral problems. Even the best teacher will spend most of her time simply getting the class to be quiet, never mind trying to actually teach[6].

Liberal philosophy has dominated public school education policy for decades: a philosophy that needs to create an equal playing field within the public school systems to make up for the inequities in the home lives of the students. This is a belief I used to hold—before I actually got into the classroom to teach. Had we, at The School embraced the same philosophy, students like Casey (and the others like him that left or were expelled) would have been allowed to stay—and unfortunately allowed to cause more havoc in the classroom. The point is that his behavior was bringing other students down. In trying to level the playing field, liberals are bringing the level of competition down to the lowest common denominator. They certainly do not mean to do so (that was never my intent, at least, I wanted to raise the standards, believing every child could meet them!). But, unfortunately, the dumbing down of the educational playing field is the result of liberal philosophy in the public schools. Teachers, administrators, government agencies cannot fix the problems that kids have at home.

When I first came to that realization, it felt like I was giving up; it felt like I was turning my back on my own ideals. But that is the ultimate failure of liberalism. It is far too idealistic and ignores the harsh realities that exist. Ideals are to be aspired to—not to be taken as policy. Kids like Casey need to be dealt with, but we have to start taking a different approach, not the liberal approach which excuses and justifies his behavior because of his home life. It doesn't help Casey and it definitely doesn't help his classmates. Rather than a free pass to misbehave, children need structure and discipline. If we really want true equality under the law (another liberal goal I firmly support as a libertarian), every child needs to be treated the same in the classroom. They need to be held to the same expectations, the same standards. If the child cannot meet those standards the bar should not be lowered for him simply because we feel sorry for him. When standards are lowered and bad behavior excused, you create a person who begins to have no sense of self-sufficiency or responsibility. In the natural lottery of life (to borrow from Rawls) we do not always win; it is not fair, but those who get the unlucky tickets in life need to work harder to achieve and compete with others in society. I am not advocating that these unlucky and unfortunate do not need or deserve help—I am saying that the help we are currently giving them isn't actually helping. I equate social welfare to the ancient adage: give a man a fish and he will eat for a day, teach a man to fish and he will eat for a lifetime. Liberals have the government handing out fish faster than society can eat them.

Unfortunately, the Conservatives don't have it right, either. They don't know how to handle kids like Casey any more than the liberals do. We had the luxury of being selective with our students; the public schools don't have that luxury. That's where Casey went upon leaving us.

Even though I have moved on from teaching, I am still enraged when I hear people blame the teachers. Or when the teachers blame the parents. Or when everyone just blames the system. We're all so busy playing the blame game, and using it to fuel our own political agendas, we forget that as we bicker, the education system as a whole becomes worse and our future potential as a nation is being slowly eroded like a sand dune being worn down by the pounding waves. We spend so much time bickering and blaming we don't deal with the kids like Casey, who are drowning, and taking the others down with them.

I still believe in Rawls' version of a just society. I believe a just and fair society does provide a safety net for its most poor and disadvantaged citizens that allows them to achieve a base standard of living, a position from which they can fairly compete. I simply no longer believe that it is the *government's* job to provide it. Our government is bankrupting itself trying to save every citizen—and seldom really helping them.

I firmly believe after my teaching experiences that people will not starve if the government discontinues food stamps. I know there are good people in our country that will use their own resources to provide for those in need. I've seen it.

Through the positive and the negative, I came to see, in my year of AmeriCorps service that there really are some people who take advantage of the state welfare system. Some people are too stubborn and set in their ways to change; others are too ignorant to know how to change or that there is actually any other way. There are people who are complacent and those who feel entitled to full aid because of a social wrong that they perceive has been done to them (even if it was done before they were born). But there are also good people, for whom the safety net has become simply a net. However, they are not encouraged to seek extra education that would give them better jobs with better salaries because the difference in salary wouldn't cover their cost of living (this was a common complaint among parents). The School is ultimately successful because it does not rely on the government—it relies on the generosity and goodness of citizens.

Ultimately, I am a libertarian because I believe in the primacy of the right of the individual, that a limited government can do a better job of governing, and that our tax dollars are better spent helping to educate people, giving them hope and something to live FOR, rather than just keep them alive. Libertarianism embodies those values of individualism in which I so strongly believe, while leaving behind both the liberal ideas of social reform that have failed so miserably and the conservative denial of the social conditions that make it impossible for many to succeed.

I guess I am too young to be conservative—but I've seen enough of harsh realities that now that I'm not a liberal. I'm still my mom's little free radical at times (I haven't lost all of my idealistic tendencies, and I kind of hope I never will). I understand now what Winston Churchill (and my dad) meant. When you are young and have had minimal exposure to the nasty, stupid, mean things that people do to themselves and one another, your natural sympathies make you want to save the world. Your energy and education make you believe you can do it. When you are older and have seen more stupidity and meanness than anyone should, and you're too tired to fight any longer, you're willing to let the world rot, so long as it leaves you alone.

This is an exaggeration, of course, but the feelings associated with my words are very real. Right now, I'm in the middle. I'm old enough to have seen some bad things, but young enough to still care. My sympathy is tempered with reason. I can't save them all—I'll kill myself trying (and I *still* would, that's why I decided NOT to pursue a career in education). I'm still convinced I can change the world (I'm now in law school) but I'm a little more realistic about the fact that I can't save it from itself—or from well-intentioned people like me who have not yet experienced the "real world".

I have a new quote, now, that I love, and that I think describes me well: "I wake up every morning determined both to change the world and have one hell of a good time. Sometimes this makes planning the day a little difficult." EB White.

End Notes

1.   The actual quote is: "If you're not a liberal at twenty, you have no heart. If you're not a conservative at forty, you have no brain."

2.   This was an inside joke between my mother and me—she watched a news show describing how free radicals in the air could cause skin damage, etc. She thought the name was cute and fit my personality.

3.   Most of my ideas and ideology surrounding the concept of a "safety net" come from the philosopher John Rawls, specifically his work entitled, *A Theory of Justice.*

4.   Most of the students, even the ones with high averages, came back for evening study anyway because it provided them with a quiet and structured environment in which to do their work, with the added benefit of being able to receive help from the teachers.

5.   That hour and a half between sports and evening study was supposed to be teacher me-time; and we were all very upset when a student was not picked up on time. It was even worse when they weren't picked up after evening study. Sometimes we would have to stay until 10:00 at night for a late parent—always the same offenders.

6.   There is an excellent article recently published in the *Los Angeles Times* describing this very situation. It is entitled "The Myth of the Extraordinary Teacher" and describes what it is like to teach in this kind of environment.
http://www.latimes.com/news/opinion/commentary/la-oe-herman-class-size-20110731,0,3910343.story.

Photo by Kalyan Varma

Russell Nelson
Research Engineer, Clarkson University; Potsdam, NY

Russell is proud to be a humble Quaker, a libertarian, and a former socialist. He lives in Potsdam, NY with his wife, Heather, and son, Eric, a BA/MA candidate in math at the State University of New York (SUNY), Potsdam. His daughter, Rebecca Nelson Jacobs, is a PhD candidate in sociology at University of Connecticut. Both children were home-schooled and on the President's List in college. Russell is currently a Research Engineer at Clarkson University. He may be contacted at <russnelson@gmail.com> or 315-600-8815.

Giving up the Granola
by
Russell Nelson

I remember voting Libertarian back in 1980, for Ed Clark. I was an inchoate voter at the time, however, and voted Democrat for quite a while after that. I had fallen into a progressive crowd and of course adopted their mores and morals. I don't remember if I even voted in 1984 or 1988. By 1992, I had learned enough about economics that I knew that neither the Democrats nor Republicans echoed my views. I've voted Libertarian ever since.

My friends, upon graduating from college and moving to Oregon, were granola-eating, sandal-wearing, long-hair, co-op shopping, tai-chi practicing lefties. After falling in with that set of friends, it would be difficult to hear any contradictory voices to the usual "we need government to protect us." I stayed there for two years, and then moved back to a college town (Potsdam) in New York. In Potsdam I joined the food co-op and found the same crowd of people.

My wife and I decided to start a family in 1985, and went religion-shopping. Based on their pacifism, we chose the Religious Society of Friends (Quakers). The main message I got from Quakers was that naturally you would be a socialist because Jesus was a socialist and all Quakers are socialists. So I dutifully bought the usual tracts, like *Food First* and read the usual journals such as *The Nation* and *Utne Reader*. I started going to the Quaker Gathering. There, I found a practicing and observant Quaker who was, dash it all, NOT a socialist. He was a libertarian, although he didn't self-identify as such, preferring instead the term "classic liberal." He was a University of Boulder economist retiree name of John P. (Jack) Powelson.

I first met Jack through his writing. We began corresponding, and I eventually became the publisher of his online journal, the "Classic Liberal Quaker," later renamed "The Quaker Economist." The online journal lived on for a few issues after Jack's death with a different editor, but is currently moribund. It was clear to me that Jack was both obedient to God's will, and was also a libertarian, respecting people's freedom consistently. Through his testimony, I realized that the proper way to protect people from corporations, serve the poor and downtrodden, wage peace, and seek equality, was through freedom, not government action.

Alas, far too many Quakers worship at the feet of Big Brother. I was just at a meeting today where the Koch Brothers were accused of being the force behind the Tea Party; where the *rich* were set against the *middle class* and the *poor*; where corporations were misbehaving because they didn't pay enough taxes (although people did acknowledge that they were obeying the law with all its tax deductions); where Republicans were conducting dark conspiracies against *the people* to advance the aims of *the rich*. I'm simply aghast that the fellow members of my society could be so gullible and unable to think for themselves.

This week, while I am at the Quaker Gathering, I have to be a closeted libertarian. I know that if I advocated for libertarian policies, nobody would want to talk to me, because I would be THAT FRUITCAKE OVER IN THE CORNER. You know, the guy nobody wants to spend any time with. It makes me sad. But, I can and do try to make the best of this situation by defending libertarians from the worst of the slanders. One fellow said to me that he had been to Tea Party events, and they're all racist libertarians. I was completely nonplussed. I should have asked him if the black Tea Party members were also racists.

My goals in life haven't changed. I still think it's important to protect the poor. I just don't think the government does a good job of that. And speaking for myself only, God tells me to actually help, not do things that have the appearance of helping, like minimum wage laws. Oh, and I still wear Birkenstocks and eat granola. Helps me blend in.

Hugo Newman
PhD Student in Political Philosophy, University College, Dublin, Ireland

My name is Hugo Newman. I am twenty-five years old. I was born and raised in Limerick, Ireland, and grew up in a picturesque tourist town called Adare. I received my primary education at Shountrade National School, and attended secondary school at Crescent College Comprehensive in Dooradoyle, Limerick. I enrolled in a BA program at Mary Immaculate College in 2004, majoring in English and philosophy, and graduating with a First Class Honors degree in 2008. The following year I entered the Masters program in philosophy at the University College, Dublin (UCD), graduating with First Class Honors in 2009. Curious about my capacity for real-life work, I was accepted for a position in a print shop in Dublin City for a year. When my curiosity was satisfied and I realized my capacity for real-life work was severely limited, I decided to return to the shores of academia and started the tedious process of applying for research funding. To my great relief, I got it right first time, and I am about to undertake a PhD in political philosophy at UCD. My interests include Ronaldinho (Brazilian footballer and master of the flip-flap), the music of Leonard Cohen, and disinfecting human and non-human surfaces.

Where You End Up When You Take a Left(y) Out of Limerick
by
Hugo Newman*

I was probably 12 or 13 when "politics" first came to my attention, albeit as a subject of derision. My brother (four years my senior) and I would get a great kick out of ridiculing those we referred to as "gimpy students" (gimpy meant something like pretentious)—the types who hung out in cafes shamelessly and not quietly declaring their political convictions. If we had been shown then what I would eventually turn in to, I'd probably have vomited on my shoes, and incurred a thrashing from my brother. Twelve years on, I'm a 25-year-old about to undertake a PhD in political philosophy. I enjoy loitering in pretentious cafes, and I habitually lose the run of myself when it comes to political talk. The story of my transition isn't particularly exciting, and although I'm sure it would profit much from some embellishment, I will try to resist the temptation to over-rationalize my actions. The choices I faced could hardly be called dilemmas. My decisions were very rarely based on the application of logic alone. My scant successes and numerous failures weren't particularly inspiring. The only thing that might be called interesting is the trajectory. I was once not just a "person of the Left", but a card-carrying socialist (I spent a year as a member of the Socialist Youth Branch in Limerick, Ireland). Now I'm a raving capitalist dog. The following is the story of that transition and, if not the reasoning that led to it, then at least the reasons I am now happy about it.

My general indifference to and occasional cynicism about politics persisted until I was perhaps 19 or 20. I studied philosophy and literature at Mary Immaculate College in my hometown of Limerick, Ireland. My aforementioned brother had undertaken a business degree at the University of Limerick when he was 18 but dropped out after two uninspiring years. He then took philosophy and literature the year before I began. Our interests had always been consonant, although while he was more drawn to literature, I was hugely taken with philosophy. Nevertheless, I have him to thank for most of the ideas I have encountered since. His guidance was invaluable.

In my first year there were times when I read almost voraciously, but most of my library time was spent posturing. I liked the idea of being "intellectual". So I acquainted myself with the big ideas and the big thinkers. Inevitably, Noam Chomsky came up. One of my lecturers was a leftist kind—a really fine man and fine teacher. He had an excellent English accent too, which helped. It was partly through him that I came to the leftist way of thinking. But it was Chomsky who really shook me up. My brother and I bought the book *Understanding Power*, a kind of Chomsky 101. For the first time politics wasn't complete drivel. It was written in relatively normal language (with just enough jargon to keep me interested), common sense, rigor, and consistency.

Politics until that point had seemed to be about the following: a handful of political parties with mysterious policy differences which for some reason could never be coherently articulated; local men in ill-fitting suits getting the potholes in your road filled; election posters that made you want to scoop out your eyeballs so you had the double pleasure of not having to look at them as well as having something to throw at them; parents getting into arguments about, well, nothing, over and over again; radio interviews by disgruntled presenters with blindsided self-promoters who resorted to equivocations like "In actual fact . . . at this moment in time . . . taken in context" and "if you look at the bigger picture", the bigger picture inevitably being another litany of equivocations. Chomsky raised questions about the nature of the political system itself, its justification (if any), the effects of political and economic institutions, the nature of power, the unofficial records of governments, the assumptions we bring to bear on political discourse. In other words, Chomsky handled words like "democracy", "justice", "right", and "truth" as though they were endangered species. Politicians on the other hand, and those who typically claimed to be "political", treated these words as though they were pests to be batted aside at the earliest opportunity.

It was Chomsky's palpable moral seriousness, paired with the near-incredible horror of government records on human rights violations that compelled me to read more. His moral-political critiques and putative solutions seemed so intuitive and basic as to be irrefutable. Clearly, the system in place in "Western" countries was not working—neither for a significant proportion of the native populations, nor for people of non-western territories who were unfortunate (or foolish) enough to partake of political/economic relations with Western countries. Poverty, pollution, corrupt politicians, corporate-state collusion, huge inequalities in wealth, imperialistic foreign policies, were all prevalent and apparently becoming more problematic. What was the name we habitually gave to the system in Western countries? Capitalist, of course. Therefore, Capitalism was not working.[1]

This seemed perfectly in line with experience. Walking around the streets of Limerick, I would see homeless people huddled in doorways, and not two seconds later be confronted by the sight of some grand, plushly decked-out business headquarters. Such everyday juxtapositions seemed to perfectly corroborate the crude syllogism which Chomsky's writings essentially endorsed: premise 1—homeless man has no money; premise 2—big business owner has lots of money; conclusion—therefore, homeless man has no money *because* big business owner has lots of money. In other words, what was going on was simply theft on a mass scale, albeit in a covert and convoluted manner.

Chomsky's solution? Seize the big business owners' property and wealth, transfer it to the workers under a democratic framework, and allow them to use the resources/wealth as they see fit—presumably, in more benevolent, wise, collectively responsible ways. Surely this was a reasonable demand? After all, all Chomsky was really calling for was the extension of the democratic mandate to *all* aspects of life, including the "purely" economic realm. And surely democracy—the pride of the West, the warm afterglow of the Enlightenment, the feather in the political cap of civilization—could not be denied without at the same time tacitly advocating a return to barbarism?

No, Chomsky was surely right. It all seemed so appealing, so commonsensical. Finally people would have a say in what really mattered. This explained everything. It explained the overwhelming apathy of people in relation to political issues. Their indifference and confusion was a symptom of their ultimate lack of control over their own destinies. Their working life would now have real meaning, since they would have democratic "control" over how their workplace was run. The poor, sick, and starving would be taken care of for good, since all resources would be harnessed according to "need rather than profit" (apparently, democratically-run workplaces did not need to concern themselves with profit, for some unexplained reason . . . .). Surely this was the answer. Not only was it both morally and materially appealing, but it also seemed to account for my own erstwhile cynicism with respect to all things political. What's more, I could now render a judgment on the prevailing political system from the outside while being spared the humiliation of entering into the mind-numbing ambiguities of everyday political talk.

With my mind primed for leftist solutions, it wasn't long before I was drawn to the Socialist Youth branch in Limerick city. I attended a few meetings and debates. Admittedly, from the outset I wasn't enamored of the few people involved in the party. Notwithstanding my personality qualms, I joined the branch out of something like a sense of duty—what, after all, would Chomsky have said if he were to see me hypocritically shun taking action? It wasn't long before I was encouraged/harangued out onto the streets every week or two to hand out slogan-ridden pamphlets (meant to appeal to "young people" and "workers" . . . not to middle-aged business owners/management types though. Apparently they were scum beyond reason), hold up placards, and serve the socialist cause in many other mortifying ways. Gradually this kind of work began to wear me down. One evening in particular took the wind out of my sails. Word came down from the central committee (or whatever it was called) that we were to canvass some of the poorer housing estates in the city. Reluctantly (and with not a small amount of terror) I obliged. Every person I talked with without exception was *at least* dismissive (some were pretty angry). Everyone seemed so disinterested, so cynical, so unreasonably distracted by their own lives and commitments. How on earth were we supposed to change *everyone's* minds, and transform people into more communally-spirited, less self-absorbed citizens?

Eventually it struck me that this wasn't actually what was in principle required for a socialist revolution. All that was required was for a *majority* to be persuaded, not even what might be called a significant majority. Then, regardless of what the rest of society wanted or thought, the socialist transformation could be pushed through. This was probably the first line of reasoning that led me to question the moral basis for socialism. Surely, regardless of what end was envisioned or promised, to *force* people to participate in socialist transformation was basically wrong?

Which led me to my second line of doubt. Wasn't it possible that many "ordinary workers" were simply happy to be ordinary workers? Even I, a card-carrying socialist, was daunted by the prospect of daily contributing to the management of the entire economy in the inevitable socialist future, either directly or indirectly through representation. I was working in a car-park during my college/leftist years. But even then I had no interest whatsoever in having more of a say in how my workplace was run, how things should be organized, how revenue should be spent and distributed, etc. I was happy to simply work the customer service desk for a significantly lower wage than management. It seemed intuitively reasonable and indeed fair. The burden of responsibility involved in managing seemed tremendous, even if it were to be shared among other employees, and even if it was just a lowly car-park I was working in. Imagine then an entire economy!

No doubt socialists would retort that the burden would be much lessened given the wholesale participation of *all* workers across the board and in every sector in such "democratic" decision-making. But this kind of answer would only raise further questions. First of all, how are *more* people and *more* opinions going to make things any less fraught or complicated? Surely, the more people that are involved, the *greater* the chances of disagreements, impasses, and production-impeding disputes arising?

191

Secondly, if democratic vote is to be the mechanism whereby decisions are reached in all economic matters, both at a national and local level, then who is to set the agenda on which the vote is to be made in the first place? Should the agenda itself be democratically decided upon? But then who decides what items are to be included as possible items for the agenda? Surely this leads to an infinite regress, whereby, if we are to be consistent, no decision can ever be (wholly) democratically reached! Wouldn't we require some non-democratic staring point?

Moreover, to delegate responsibility to some elected representatives would seem no more attractive a prospect. For one, what would the incentive be for a prospective socialist manager to take on the huge burden of responsibility involved in planning if they would, presumably, be subject to instant recall should they be deemed unsuited to the task? Surely no one would want to take on such an extra burden without some kind of material compensation? But then any such reward system would seem to fly in the face of the whole raison d'être of socialism. And assuming no such reward system was in place, it's hard to see how it would not be the most politically manipulative who would tend to rise to positions of decision-making authority in the socialist economy. After all, it would not necessarily be the most productively rational, but rather the most *popular* (presumably majoritarian) production policy which would tend to win out.

Would there not then arise tensions *between* industries, given the limited resources available in society with which to realize the various production processes? And to this extent, would not the most popular elected managers tend to be those who could garner (or at least convincingly promise) the best materials/conditions for the workers in the various companies? But how would such planners gain the upper hand in competition for highly demanded or undifferentiated resources? Surely, on the basis of socialist morality, each person's claim is as valid as the next person's. Will such decisions not ultimately have to be delegated to some (ideally) solomonistic, benign final decision-maker(s), who would be immune to all iniquitous advances/offers from subordinate elected managers who seek what they and their industrial constituents demand? Are we then to pin our hopes for a functioning socialist economy on such a wise final decision-making entity being always at hand? And what then is to stop an implacable bureaucracy from coalescing, assuming that the ultimate decision-makers would have the final word on even policing and judicial matters? Are we to simply assume and blindly hope that wise benevolence will suddenly and instantly become the norm once the socialist revolution has been pushed through? Granted not all of these thoughts came to my mind at once, nor in such a neat fashion. But these were the *kinds* of doubts I was beginning to entertain.

After I completed my degree in my hometown, I enrolled in a masters degree in philosophy program at the University College, Dublin. At this point, I was beginning to relish the thought of having a legitimate excuse for divorcing myself from the socialist branch in my hometown, even if I didn't want to admit it to myself or others. I felt increasingly repulsed by the kind of work involved. I told my comrades that I wasn't going to be able to stay involved since I was moving city and would be very busy with my course work. I'll never forget how surprised I was at how relieved I felt when I left that last branch meeting, even if it was tempered by a pang of guilt. But the relief was undeniable, and bolstered by a growing sense that my nascent moral and practical reservations about socialism were basically justified.

In my new studies, my eye was drawn to one module in particular, "Law, Liberty, and the State", given by Professor Gerard Casey. Beforehand I had heard mutterings associating Professor Casey with "the right", "neo-liberal ideas", "unbridled capitalism", etc., etc. Still a lefty in spirit (albeit one with considerable doubts), I took the course half out of curiosity, half out of a haughty belief that I could still meet any arguments adduced in favor of capitalism. Of course I could—it was CAPITALISM after all! Dirty, rotten, greedy, crass, manipulative, polluting, exploitative capitalism. Who could even *consider* defending it!? Clearly we were living under it, and clearly it wasn't working for the majority of people. What's more, all the most intelligent and righteous academics were on my side—Chomsky, Finkelstein[2], Zinn, and their seemingly endless retinue of intelligent disciples in humanities departments the world over. Who in their right mind would take on an intellectual army of that caliber and magnitude? Clearly this Casey guy was a crackpot.

Much to my initial shock, Casey was entirely reasonable, remarkably articulate, and utterly convincing. The seminar was, at the risk of hyperbole, mind-shattering in the most productive sense of the term. Casey, via Rothbard and others in the libertarian tradition, uprooted countless of my most deep-seated yet intellectually malignant assumptions. Taking in economics, politics, and ethics, Casey's unwavering defense regularly elicited slack-jawed reactions from the class. Some seemed downright disgusted. And yet tellingly, the characteristic retort from those taking the seminar was either an incredulous scoff or an outright evasion of the issue at hand. No matter how compelled some seemed to be by the logical rigor of Casey's arguments, they still could not bear to bring themselves to accept his conclusions. Some therefore found themselves agreeing "logically", but disagreeing by some other standard—typically by appeal to emotional reservations.

I am reminded here of Walter Block's invocation of evolutionary psychology in explaining why people often seem so naturally averse to libertarian ideas. In the distant past, humans would typically have lived in much smaller packs/tribes. These groups would have survived by and large by sharing and engaging in what Block calls "explicit" cooperation, long before the advent of complex exchange economies. As such, those individuals and groups who cultivated strong empathetic impulses tended to survive over those with weaker impulses.

Indirect/monetary exchange economies emerged relatively late in human evolution. People were not yet "hard-wired" or naturally selected for appreciation of the advantages of indirect or *implicit* cooperation through the pricing mechanism. Much in the same way as people nowadays are still more afraid of snakes than of bathtubs (despite bathtubs being the cause of many more deaths than snakes), so people are now much more inclined to see the pursuit of profit as antithetical to human progress rather than as essential to it, given that it *seems* to be an *exclusively* self-serving behavior.

With this in mind, it is perhaps not surprising that many who took Casey's class came out of it in the untenable position of conceding the logical rigor of the arguments while rejecting their conclusions. I don't mean to suggest that I wasn't among those who at first turned away from the conclusions required by reason. I came round only slowly, and rather reluctantly. In retrospect, the very fact that I was so reluctant now strikes me as a further testament to the truth of austro-libertarian ideas. I was ultimately compelled, much against my own emotional and psychological tendencies, to accept the arguments Casey, Rothbard, and others advanced. After all, I now had to say that I thought Chomsky et. al. were wrong in many respects, a claim which would no doubt provoke charges of arrogance and pretension.

Timing can be crucial. In my case, I was fortunate enough (in the glass half-full sense) to be taking Casey's course at the exact time of the onset of the global financial crisis in 2008. Fortunate, because it was in large part the Austrian School's ability to satisfactorily explain the crisis which finally convinced me that austro-libertarianism was not just correct, but vitally so. I was all too familiar with the Marxist refrain that capitalism was law-bound to self-destruct due to internal contradictions. The problem was that the Marxists and socialists never seemed able to account for either the timing or the specific features of the crisis. The theoretical work of Mises, Hayek, and others comprehensively explained both of these aspects.

The artificial credit expansion and correspondingly lower-than-market-level interest rates induced by both the European Central Bank and Federal Reserve System in the United States in the years leading up to the crisis drew resources into higher-order stages of production such as construction. However, the increased investment in these industries was not offset by a complementary abstention from consumption by consumers. Therefore, prices in the higher order stages rose to a point where those who had taken out large loans to finance their property speculation could no longer afford to pay them back. Both those on the Left and in the mainstream typically resorted to question-begging appeals to such factors as "greed", "under-regulation", "irrational behavior", "overly complex financial instruments", and of course "unbridled capitalism", in their attempts to explain the crisis. However, none of these putative explanations could withstand even the most cursory scrutiny. The identification of "greed" as the cause merely begged the question of why we got so greedy when we did. Why did we get so greedy in the years leading up to the global crisis rather than, say, in the 1970s, or the early 90s, or any other time for that matter? Moreover, why did we all seem to "get greedy" in concert, so that thousands of bankers, speculators, businessmen, and government officials the world over were systematically misled into making/facilitating imprudent or excessively risky investment decisions over the same period and in the same direction? Neither was the appeal to a "lack of regulation" enough; for even if we were to suppose that more regulations would have effectively interrupted the process (a dubious claim in itself), this would still not explain why people had been tempted into property speculation to an "irrational" degree in the first place, such that regulation in the financial and property sectors was more urgently needed than in other sectors.

Here in Ireland, these kinds of charges go on unabated in the mainstream media to this day. Ireland's relative lack of a libertarian tradition of any kind certainly has not helped to stem the tide of nonsense that passes for analysis. However, with the advent of the Internet, such factors are becoming much less decisive. In my own case, my deep commitment to libertarian ideas may not have come about so soon were it not for the dedication and generosity of those who set up, maintain, and contribute to the Ludwig von Mises Institute's wonderful website, mises.org. Its vast collection of free literature and media did much to accelerate my liberation from the intellectual fetters of socialism.

Indeed, I will conclude my remarks on this theme. The Internet is of course merely another medium for the exchange of information—albeit a very powerful one—and is no more naturally conducive to the propagation of correct ideas than any other medium. In this respect the

Internet is somewhat akin to a market economy. In a free market, people won't *necessarily* pursue what you or I might consider to be honorable ends. A free market is only as "moral" as those who constitute it. And yet, in the spirit of glass half-fullery, I am inclined to take this as a source of encouragement rather than as a cause for concern. We have now an unprecedented opportunity to take full responsibility for these ideas and convey them to others in a great many novel ways. Mises.org is leading the way in this regard. Freedom is a powerful thing, but only for those who are willing to take responsibility for themselves and their beliefs. This is what we must do.

*Hugo Newman is a recipient of a Government of Ireland Postgraduate Scholarship from the Irish Research Council for the Humanities and Social Sciences.

End Notes

1.   I do not mean to impute such a simplistic argument to Chomsky. Rather, this passage is supposed to be reflective of my own initially simplistic reading of his work. Nevertheless, although Chomsky's picture is more eloquently filled in, I believe that the basic misidentification is still there in his writings—namely, the mistaking of the surface phenomena of Western market economies (or what is left of the market after government is done with it!) for the root causes of the problems listed above. As Mises, Rothbard and other Austrian School economists have definitively demonstrated, it is rather state actions/interference and the economic havoc they wreak which are in the overwhelming majority of cases the root cause of the problems listed above.

2.   I feel compelled to mention here that, although I now no doubt radically diverge from Finkelstein on matters of ideology, I remain a great admirer of his vital critical works exposing and unequivocally condemning US and Israeli government crimes. He has been a great inspiration and deserves, in my opinion, the highest intellectual and moral respect for his work to date.

Scott Rhymer
Freelance Writer and Doctoral Candidate in Modern
American and European History, University of New
Mexico; Albuquerque, NM

Scott Rhymer is a freelance writer and doctoral candidate in Modern American and European History at the University of New Mexico. His focus has been on British and Italian imperialism, and most recently on the impact of science fiction on the development of technology and modern American culture. He is a former intelligence analyst and former soldier. He lives in Albuquerque, New Mexico with his wife and daughter.

Pursuing Freedom
by
Scott Rhymer

As a child, I was exposed to a sort of soft international socialism that my mother espoused. She was a child of postwar Scotland, where the economy collapsed as shipbuilding and other industries moved away to the south (England) or disappeared entirely. Moving to Pennsylvania, we settled in the Lehigh Valley, in the 1970s still a major industrial area. However, within a decade International, Mack Trucks, Bethlehem Steel, and most of the other major manufacturers had pulled up stumps and headed for places with more forgiving tax rates, if they survived at all. That provided a backdrop to the liberal (read "Progressive") ideas that I was raised with: companies were screwing over workers and then closing the plants after people gave their lives to them without leaving them much to fall back on.

From early on, I was a fan of science fiction. It fit with the image of humankind and society as "perfectible" that permeates Progressive thinking. Technology, reason, and a bit of prodding, it seemed could make people *better*. People were simply ignorant of what they really needed and what was best for them. Progressivism promised a society where people were treated fairly, where everyone would be cared for at the most basic levels, at least. (The idea of what is basic, of course, varies from person to person ... from those that think this means a hovel and a bowl of rice a day, to those who assume the government will be providing a person with steaks for dinner and a Bentley in every driveway.) Capitalism extolled greed and an "unfair" society—one where everyone would be unequal, and racism was an assumed, vestigial stain on the nation due to slavery. How could a society with these obvious defects be good?

For me, the first cracks in the Progressive facade appeared while I was living in Philadelphia in my early twenties. The subject of racism came up, and like a good Progressive soldier I started aping the party line regarding the racism inherent in American society. One of my black coworkers, hearing me and one of the younger black kids complaining, proceeded to set us straight: We had no clue, we were told, what real racism was. He had grown up in 1950s Mississippi where a black man could be murdered with impunity simply because of the color of his skin. At that time, he reminded us, any black man could find a job if he wanted, and if he worked hard, could get ahead. The racism that we were seeing, we were informed, was much more insidious—it was a self-hating racism that saw blacks as somehow without agency, unable to improve themselves without the helping hand of a government that didn't care about them beyond how they voted (if they voted).

It had never occurred to me that there were "conservative" blacks. It made me look foolish, having my assumptions rattled, and rightfully so.

Another point of contention was the attitude toward self-defense. In Philadelphia then, violent crime was rampant in my neighborhood. Not having been raised to protect myself ("Violence never solves anything!"), I realized that I was at a disadvantage. A weapon could balance the field in the event of an attack. Those "liberal" friends of mine, even my family, didn't "get" my desire for a weapon—not to go out and pick fights, but to stop them from happening in the first place. I was expected to rely on the police, who were not present when they were needed. I should just give a criminal my money or property—it's just stuff, after all! It was at this time I realized that you don't get to opt out of elements of the Progressive agenda; you have to accept the package *in toto*.

A series of personal failures and unemployment caused me to reexamine myself as the '90s began. I realized that the failures I had experienced were not the result of impersonal forces, society, or other people ... any success or failure in my life was, ultimately, my fault. This acceptance of personal responsibility, I think, was where my path with Progressivism, or "the Left" began to diverge. I knuckled down, returned to college, got a job, and rebuilt my life on the notion that I had to make my success. I couldn't hope that someone else would do it for me.

In the mid-1990s I joined the military as an intelligence analyst and got to see what the world really looked like outside the United States. The international agencies that were supposed to make life better did nothing of the sort. International banks locked poor nations into perpetual dependence, much as my former coworker in Philadelphia had blamed government welfare for the collapse of the black family. International peacekeepers did not save Bosnians from the mass graves; like the police, they came along after the fact and brought people (sometimes) to trial. Sometimes they simply looked the other way, as in Rwanda. My country didn't steal food from the needy, like the officials in Somalia; our justice system didn't cut a thief's hand off as is done in Saudi Arabia. These experiences convinced me that the image of my nation I was sold did not fit with what I was seeing. If anything, the United States provided an environment in which people were (usually) safe in their life and property, where you could get a job and get ahead if you worked hard, and which attempted to do good around the world, even if it sometimes did it in a bumbling and arrogant manner.

I think I would say I didn't stop being liberal, but discovered what a *real* liberal was: a person who believes that people should be left to succeed or fail as they will, live as they will, and if they are so inclined aid people where help is wanted. As I continued my studies in American History, I came to realize that, foremost, real, classical liberalism (and by extension, it's heir, libertarianism) is about property. Proudhon was wrong. Property is not Theft ... property starts with self-ownership, and the right to be safe in your body, thoughts, labor, and, by extension, the property that is your labor made manifest. If someone, if a country, does not honor property, they cannot honor the notion that I owe myself—that I am not the property of a king, a president, or a political movement.

I call myself a libertarian for simplicity sake, but to spit in the eye of Progressives that have tainted the word liberal, I tell them I'm a "real liberal"—someone who believes that true freedom is not the liberation from responsibility, where the human being can be perfected like some piece of technology; it is the freedom of self-reliance, self-respect, and self-expression.

201

Neema James Vedadi
Television journalist and media producer; Pasco, WA

Neema Vedadi is a young television journalist and independent media producer. He won the Wyoming Association of Broadcaster's award for Best TV News Piece in 2010 and now works at a CBS affiliate in Pasco, Washington. *Guns and Weed: The Road to Freedom,* a documentary Neema co-produced, has been screened worldwide. Neema's other projects include producing libertarian hip-hop and recording a weekly podcast called "Freedom Feens". In his free time he enjoys relaxing with his wife Jessica and their two "fur-kids", an orange cat named Phlocken and a one-eyed Alaskan Malamute named Yukon. He hopes to one day raise a family in the Texas hill country.

Why I Left the Left, Hate the State, and Love Life
by
Neema James Vedadi

New reporter: "So what do you rap about?"

Me: "Well I'm an anarchist. So mostly it's about how ridiculous the government is."

New reporter: "That's weird ... being a reporter and all."

Me: "I know"

A bit of small talk with a fresh-out-of-college TV reporter who was shadowing me during a normal work day. I'm a 27-year-old TV reporter at a small market station in Tri-Cities, Washington. It's a living (though not much of one), but my real passions are advocating freedom and producing hip-hop. At my day job I'm constrained by the status-quo narrative expected of a mainstream reporter. In my free time I'd describe myself as a radical. I strike at the root. I've co-produced a documentary film called *Guns and Weed: The Road to Freedom*; I get to explain my real reaction to current events in a weekly podcast with my friend Michael W. Dean called "Freedom Feens"; and my libertarian hip-hop anthem "I Own Me" tells the government explicitly to back off.

While the media I make in my free time fully rejects the need for a government, I haven't always felt that way. I grew up wanting to be president. I thought I could help the disenfranchised with public policy. I voted Democrat. . . . Hell, I *believed* in voting. My dad has a PhD in economics and voted for Obama. My mom was a public school teacher who always voted Democrat. My dad came to America from Iran a few years before the Islamic revolution; like most Iranian immigrants I've met in America he is non-religious. From a very early age I always had an interest in my Iranian heritage and the history and geo-politics of the Middle East. During the Bush years this developed into an antiwar sentiment that felt at home with the Left. But I eventually left the Left and then abandoned all mainstream political thinking. Here's the story of how I got here, how I struggle in a world where questioning the status quo is taboo, and where I hope I, and human society, can go from here.

Earliest Memories of Politics

Like many American kids I was taught to love the government from a very early age. Public school usually gets most of the blame for this. But even though I started off my education at a private school I wasn't spared the indoctrination. My school was named "Challenger" after the NASA tragedy and every morning we vowed our submission to the federal government by saying the Pledge of Allegiance.

One of my earliest memories was going with my mom to vote. I was four and it was the 1988 presidential election. I knew enough to ask mom who she voted for. She said "everyone who is a Democrat." She explained to me those were the people who helped the poor and unfortunate. Her oversimplification made sense to me then.

Of course George H. W. Bush won that election, which lead to my first memories of America going to war. During "Desert Storm" I saw my friends with yellow ribbons and "support the troops" paraphernalia. At the grocery story I tried to get my mom to buy me a "patriotic" trinket. She wouldn't buy it and when I got upset she explained that the troops had killed some friends of daddy. Another maternal oversimplification to be sure, but it hit me hard. I didn't want anything to do with war cheerleading anymore and I knew that the old skinny man in the Oval office was a bad guy.

During my childhood there was some foreshadowing of my eventual rejection of mainstream partisan politics. I though Ross Perot was awesome. I was only nine but watching him on TV spoke to me. His charts and graphs about the deficit made sense. I would regurgitate his speeches and my family would laugh and ask me to do the Ross Perot impression again.

Around that time my parents divorced and my mother and I headed to her home town of Pasadena, Texas. Pasadena and the surrounding area is a mostly lower middle class suburb of the Houston ship channel. My mom had grown up there the daughter of a hard working Italian immigrant. Most of the men in Pasadena have blue collar jobs in the refineries or related industry. A few things here pushed me to identify with the Left. First, my mom had two failed marriages with two Texas rednecks (both had mullets and drove Camaros when she met them). These two step-dads both used racism against Iranians to build rapport with my mom. My mom is by no means racist but she was bitter about my dad and I would overhear these guys telling my mom that "Middle Easterners just don't know how to treat their women"

In Texas I also quickly picked up on rap. It was part of my way of rebelling against step-dad #1 who would tell me to "stop talking like some black ace-of-spades". I still have no idea what that means. But I grew reactionary against what I saw as racism. And the media told me that not being racists was lefty and it was hip and folks on the right were square and worked as highway patrol officers and oppressed us black, brown, and half-brown people.

Economic factors also pushed me to identify with the Left. Both my stepdads eventually quit their blue collar work and tried to make it as entrepreneurs. Both were really bad at it. Basically trying out the kind of schemes you see on late night TV. Stepdad #2 even became a Kirby vacuum cleaner salesman. My mom's public school teacher's salary was the main source of income throughout many of these years. I soured on entrepreneurship as a way to make a living. I saw my mom's public school work as what fed me, in essence the state kept food on my plate. My distaste for the business sector grew more when my real dad, who had actually built a pretty successful restaurant empire in Salt Lake City, went bankrupt. He went from zipping through Utah's canyons in a Mercedes Benz SL500 convertible to getting honked at because his old Ford Aerostar wouldn't go more than 30 mph uphill. At one point I even vowed to myself that I'd never try to start my own business (now I'm vowing to do that very thing). I wanted stability and I felt a good society provides that for its citizens.

D.A.R.E. The anti-drug propaganda class in school also pushed me leftward. They gave us a sort of graphic novel/workbook explaining all the different drugs. It really made me want to smoke pot. I took a pencil and drew joints in all the characters' mouths and used a red pen to make their eyes bloodshot. I thought drugs were cool and drug warriors were lame. And in my pre-teen mind-set the left-right continuum made sense. I knew the old white squares on the right wanted to lock us up for smoking a plant.

As I entered my teen years I became more anti-authority and yet felt more a part of the Left. Now I can see the contradiction but at the time I couldn't yet conceive of a world without government.

All About Authority: High School in Texas

High school was a very statist place. Students couldn't go anywhere without special ID cards we had to wear at all times. If we were late to school we had to check into the office and fill out paper work. There was a strict dress code. Not wearing a belt could get you sent to I.S.S or "in school suspension". That's where you sit in a cubicle all day and aren't allowed to say a word to anyone else. I played football every year in high school and while in retrospect I don't find that to be a negative type of authority at all (it was voluntary and fun) the pep rallies did condition us for a pack mentality. Everything was about school spirit and the collective.

I actually loved it though. I ran for senior class president. My campaign poster had a picture of me with a Mohawk, wearing a wifebeater tank-top, holding my infant brother. The caption read "won't somebody please think of the children!" I won! My friends gave me a lot of encouragement. They told me I was smart and charismatic and could be the real president one day. I let it get to my head. I had dreams of grandeur. I thought to myself; "Authority isn't bad itself; our democracy just isn't working to its full potential. All the old square right wingers run things. If cool young people like me run it everything will be gravy!"

I came up with crazy ideals—like welfare sex. As a teenage boy, I thought about sex constantly. I figured it was such an important part of human life that the government should provide a prostitute to people who couldn't get laid. I also thought that voting should be mandatory. After all, the Internet was just starting to come of age. Society finally had the technology to ask the masses what they really wanted and get a better turnout than just 30 percent of the electorate. I thought the reigns of the government just needed to be better connected to the "masses." I would use words like proletariat and talk about how we needed to rise up.

Throughout high school economic reality never kept me grounded. We were required to take an economics class but our "teacher" hated the subject. She flat out told us it would be boring and she made little effort to explain anything. She just didn't care, so most of the time we would just gossip and use the class as a free period or study hall. I eventually stopped going. Not that the Keynesian stuff that was probably in the text book would have helped me anyway.

Nine-eleven also happened my senior year. As I watched I felt a welling up of statist thirst for vengeance. My first thought was that it was the Chinese. A few months before I'd heard that some American spy-plane had crashed near China. I actually daydreamed about joining up and going to war against China for downing the twin towers (this was before the media started mentioning Osama Bin Laden).

Another major impact of 9-11 was how it pushed me to my career path. I was glued to the cable news stations. Everyone was. I'm pretty sure that's when those running tickers at the bottom of the screen started . . . because people were so thirsty for as much new information as the networks could fit on the screen. I thought to myself "I want to be the one quenching people's thirst for info". I felt I was fairly smart. I had charisma. And I wanted to bring people the truth. My young self thought TV news was a perfect fit. After I graduated I headed to the University of Texas in Austin (the most liberal city in the state) to pursue a degree in Broadcast Journalism (the most liberal degree in the school . . . well after gender studies and what not).

College—Hate the Red State

In college I developed a real hatred for the folks in the White House, the military-industrial complex, and the police state. I wasn't alone; most of my friends in college felt the same way but we thought the opposite of Red State Fascism was Blue State compassion.

My opposition to the Iraq war was strong. I walked out of class and marched with thousands of others in the lead-up to the war. I remembered being young and opposing the first Desert Storm. Now

207

that I was in college I knew the Iraq war was just a corrupt power grab by Bush, Cheney, and Halliburton.

Race issues also pushed me leftward. My friends in journalism class would always criticize the antics of the Young Conservatives of Texas, a campus club that we considered racist. I remember how ridiculous we thought they were when they held an "Affirmative Action Bake-Sale". A cookie cost $1.00 for white students, $0.50 for Hispanic students and $0.25 for black students. Now I see that they were trying to show how racist "affirmative action" truly is. However, at the time my lefty friends and I thought they were attacking an institution that was vital to "social justice"

I also got a summer job trying to raise money for Democratic presidential candidate John Kerry. While I didn't really know much about him I felt anybody would be better than Bush—especially a Democrat. That was pretty much the gist of my pitch as I would knock on somebody's door, I would ask them if they wanted to donate any money to help make Bush a one-term president. It worked a fair amount of the time and I actually felt like I was doing some good.

College is also where I began getting into music. I'd always loved rap growing up in Houston. And Austin bills itself as the "live music capitol of the world," many people I knew were in a band. I began free-styling more at parties and writing my own songs. The anti-authoritarian narrative is what really spoke to me, especially in college as more and more run-ins with the police state had me sayin' F*ck the Police.

Cops seemed to be around to keep me from having fun. I remember making out with a date in my car and the 5-0 showed up. Pulled us out of the car and made us both wait for half an hour in the cold while they searched the car. After that I learned to never give consent to search my car. But that anti-search stance didn't work on border guards. Some friends and I took a trip to Nuevo Laredo, a Mexican border town. On our way back the border guard didn't like the duct tape on my steering wheel (my airbag had deployed months ago and I couldn't afford to have it fixed). He pulled us out of the car and searched the whole thing, complaining about the messiness of my car. He asked "why don't you ever clean your car?" I replied "because guys like you will do it for me". He wasn't amused. He confiscated a few *Hustler* magazines since apparently it was illegal to transport porn across the border. Then the guards took us into a back room where they gave us what would now be considered an "enhanced pat down." We all thought it was ridiculous and blamed the post 9-11 homeland security BS.

When I became a decent enough rapper to perform at a few small shows I always billed myself as the "lyrical terrorist". This was a jab back at anyone who'd ever called me "Bin Laden" or "sand n*gga". It was a jab at anti-Middle Eastern sentiment in general. I wrote lyrics violently lashing out at those in power like "take a congressman and stab him in the eye/till the motherfucker die". I had begun to harbor an intense distrust and disrespect of those in Washington but I still believed in politics and didn't yet understand the libertarian non-aggression principle. I was often angry and felt that force was necessary to change things.

I didn't start to truly understand freedom until after I graduated college and left the closed world of government schools for the real world. It was 2006 and Nancy Pelosi made me realize that it wasn't just Republicans who were full of sh*t.

Seeing the Real World—Taking off the Statist Goggles

The real world hit me like a ton of bricks. I had trouble finding a job in my career field. I had trouble getting motivated as well, since most of the entry level TV reporter jobs start out paying barely above the minimum wage and I was making more than $100 dollars just in tips every night at my college job of delivering pizzas. I also realized I was almost $20,000 in debt—a hefty sum for an education I didn't feel had helped me get ahead. My whole life I was told to get good grades and go to college and then I'd be successful. And after graduating at the top of my class in both high school and college I was working fast food. It was the first real hint I had that something was very off with the idea of social democracy.

In 2006 the Democrats swept into Congress on what I believed was an anti-war, anti-Bush mandate. I often tell people that Nancy

Pelosi made me a libertarian. Once she became the speaker all we got was more of the same. The long awaited Democratic Congress did nothing to curb the warfare state or the police state. I felt betrayed.

Then Congressional Democrats were able to pass a minimum wage increase. Though as a pizza delivery boy 2/3rds of my money came from tips, my hourly pay was minimum wage, so I thought "hey at least the government is giving me a raise!" This too made me realize something was wrong with the government trying to shape society. My boss sent out a letter explaining how he couldn't afford to keep up with the new minimum wage unless they raised prices. We also started charging a delivery fee to customers. The higher pizza cost and new delivery charge led to smaller tips. I actually ended up bringing in slightly less money than before the minimum wage hike! Not only that but it seemed every other business that relied on minimum wage labor also raised their prices. The cost of food at restaurants and fast food joints went up. So did the cost of clothing and other consumer goods. I realized that the government minimum wage actually made me poorer!

I felt I needed to get more informed. The lefty narrative no longer seemed to explain the real world. About that time an alternative book store called Brave New Books opened up next door to my pizza shop. I decided to check it out. They had a bunch of Ron Paul stuff. I had heard my mom mention him. She lives in his congressional district and met him in the second grade class she was teaching. She told me he had come to her school and given all the students a copy of the Constitution and then explained the principles of liberty to them. Though the guy was a Republican he seemed kind of cool and my mom, who was always a Democrat, told me she had a good feeling about him. At the book store I picked up Ron Paul's *A Foreign Policy of Freedom*.

It was a collection of his speeches in Congress against war and American interventionism—all based on the idea that government action is inherently ineffective in achieving its aims and prevents individuals from interacting peacefully. It was an epiphany for me! I had always decried the government's meddling overseas and saw the hypocrisy, but Paul was arguing that when the government takes a hands-off approach to anything it gets better because government

210

action is based on force even when its intentions seem noble. It also made tremendous sense to me that my tax dollars shouldn't go to anything I don't support. I would never voluntarily send a check to anyone to blow up civilians half way around the world, especially in an area where my family has roots. But I was forced to through taxation. And if that's wrong then it was also wrong that taxpayers paid for my education when they didn't even know me. Paul opened up a Pandora's Box of principle in my head.

I registered to vote as a Republican for the first time just to support Paul's presidential bid. I became an alternate delegate to our district convention. My friends thought I was crazy to support a Republican. I told them Paul transcended party politics, what I was really supporting was peace and freedom.

I got an office job in a cubicle right about the time Ron Paul left the 2008 presidential race. I'm on the computer all day and I start to visit Paul's new website "Campaign for Liberty". It led me to LewRockwell.com and Antiwar.com. I became immersed in a world of consistency. The unifying theory is non-aggression. Everything just sort of clicked. Violence is an immoral and ineffective way of organizing society and governments are in essence violence. Even though Congress writes laws giving themselves permission to tax us it still boils down to theft. And even though the UN writes resolutions that governments use to justify war—if it's not a truly defensive action—it usually boils down to mass murder. A person should be held to the same moral standard no matter what uniform they're wearing or what title they hold because all human interaction boils down to an individual's decisions.

Don't get me wrong, I hadn't become a pacifist. I understand people have a right to defend themselves. The key and kernel of truth and consistency for me philosophically was the "Non-Aggression Principle". Basically aggression (the unagreed upon damaging, theft, or destruction of person or property) is morally wrong, defending against it is not. If a murderer tries to take my life and I prevent that incident from occurring by taking his then I've done nothing morally wrong. In fact I've prevented an aggressive act from taking place in essence doing a good thing. But is it right to storm a former acquaintances' home because I think he has guns and might not like me? No. Then I am the aggressor and he would be right to fight back. Once this simple premise became clear it all sort of "clicked" for me and once I heard Lew Rockwell explain what being an Anarcho-Capitalist meant I was like "that's me!"

Through the "Non-Aggression Principle" I realized the whole concept of a government or a "state" as we conceive of it is immoral because it's based on aggression. If you asked me if governments have a right to defend themselves I would say that they don't have moral grounds to exist in the first place and they are by definition aggressors (unless 100% of that country's citizens completely and explicitly agreed to be a subject of that government and they all signed a contract stating they'll agree to be taxed, regulated, and killed at the whims of the rulers). If two completely volunteer armies met on a battlefield away from any possibility of collateral damage and tore each other to pieces then no aggression would have necessarily occurred, just as there's nothing wrong with two men agreeing to a duel. But modern warfare bears no resemblance to this.

About the time I was undergoing this major change in my philosophy Obama was elected president. I now expected it would be nothing more than a third Bush term. I had a bumper sticker on my car with Obama's picture on it and the caption "You're going to be disappointed". I also finally got a job in the TV news industry and was curious about how my new found political orientation would sit with my employer.

I was 24 and headed to Riverton, Wyoming to be a bureau reporter for a network affiliate there. Riverton is near the Wind River Indian Reservation. In my coverage of the "Rez" I realized how much dependence on government can hurt a society. There was no economy to speak of on the reservation. Government subsidies paid for just about everything. The tribes were just starting to make some money from a new casino which I saw as hopeful. But self-sufficiency didn't seem to even cross the tribal leader's mind. With 60 percent of all their money coming from the state and federal government (the rest from the casino and fees paid by oil and gas drillers using tribal land) I asked the tribal chairman if he ever hoped the rez would have its own self sufficient economy and not need government subsidies any more ... he answered with one word "no".

Yet Wyoming, more than any other place I can imagine, seemed welcoming to a libertarian TV reporter. Folks not on the reservation were a pretty libertarian type in a lot of ways. I did a story on how government regulations had ruined a booming uranium mining industry in the Gas Hills. Once I moved up to the main station in Casper I became the weekend anchor and was able to write and read the news with no one to edit my content! Viewers picked up on my libertarian sensibilities. In public people would say things like "you're one of the few who get it!"

During my time in Casper the Wyoming Firearms Freedom Act was passed. It actually imposed a penalty on any federal agent who infringed on the 2nd amendment rights of any Wyoming citizen possessing a gun manufactured inside the state (since the feds use interstate commerce for much of their regulatory actions). I got all the major candidates for governor at the time to give me an interview about how they would enforce it. And two of them showed up to be filmed shooting with me at the gun range.

In Wyoming I filmed my music video "I Own Me". It was mostly inspired by my reading of Bulter Shaffer's *Boundaries of Order*; a book that explained how the framework of private property allows freedom to work in the modern world and allows society to prosper. Private property starts with yourself. The concept of self ownership is simple and easy to digest. If you truly do own yourself then things like taxes and drug prohibition are obviously immoral.

Fellow freedom fighter Michael W. Dean saw the video and we built a fast friendship. He also lived in Casper and quickly taught me how to shoot and carry a gun. Since my switch to liberty I believed in the freedom of self-defense, but Dean showed me how it actually worked in the real world. During our time shooting our conversations led us to start making our independent film *Guns and Weed: The Road to Freedom*. The film is our testament to the concept that freedom is one piece. Basically your freedom to ingest whatever you want is the same as my freedom to buy whatever I want for self-defense. A crime is only committed when someone aggresses against another's property and the government seems to have the market cornered on aggression.

While Wyoming was not a libertarian paradise, my time there certainly encouraged and solidified my belief that freedom is the ultimate goal ... and all society needs to achieve it is a respect for private property and an understanding of the non-aggression principle.

When my two year contract to work at the TV station in Casper expired, I decided to continue to pursue TV news. I married my girlfriend as soon as my contract was over and took another TV reporting job in Washington state.

Marriage—Guns, Gold, and Micro-capitalism

Washington state is certainly not a friendly place for freedom. In one study it ranked 40th on a list of which states allowed the most freedom. I have definitely experienced that. Among the people here, every problem seems to come with an idea for a government solution. There is a set of state laws called the RCWs and people actually know the ones they believe are relevant to them by their "RCW numbers". You have to have a license or a permit to do just about anything and it rarely requires any type of test or class; the government just wants your money. For example, I was interested in finding other work here and was offered a job working in a casino only to find out I must buy a "gaming license" for around $400. No testing, no education required; just paper work and money.

Maybe it's this state, or maybe it's a fact of working in a bigger media market but my feelings of what journalism should be just don't fly here. I don't want to get into too much detail since I'm still under contract. Let's just say being a libertarian at a news station here feels like being a vegetarian working in a slaughterhouse. I stay sane by working on a weekly liberty podcast with Michael W. Dean called "Freedom Feens."

My wife, Jessica, also keeps me sane and grounded. She feels the oppression here as keenly as I do. She also started out as a lefty but has blended her philosophy and mine. We both thought the process of getting a government marriage license was silly and we complain together about ridiculous laws and regulations.

Jessica used to be scared of guns. My gun ownership led to a few fights before we were married. But now when I carry she's more comfortable. When we're walking and a shady character passes us she pats my hip to make sure I'm packin'.

She's also encouraged our investment in precious metals to hedge against inflation caused by the Federal Reserve System. Her dream is for us to home school our kids and have land so we can grow our own food and opt out of the government's industrial food complex. Jessica has become a dynamo at producing many of the goods we use: laundry detergent, dish washing detergent, clothing, our own almond milk, etc. I call her my micro-capitalist because she's always finding new means of production on our individual scale. With her by my side I feel like I'm already living free.

I still occasionally argue with my dad about economics, and my mom seems to have become a socialist now (although she listens to all my Freedom Feens podcasts). But I'm optimistic that I'll live to see the free society I envision. Where people interact voluntarily and peacefully through horizontal networks and the top down centralized system we call government has ceased to exist—a relic in history books like African-American slavery. I think among younger people freedom just makes more sense. They all interact through social networks on the Internet. They're more likely to believe the consensus of those they trust on Facebook more than any government agency or mainstream media source. It's hard for young people to think of the Left as cool when the Left's hero and first black president is bombing Africa without any congressional approval and ruining the economic outlook for teens and college grads. I used to see the Left as the voice of the masses against oppression, but now I realize their "hope" all rests on jackbooted thugs who make no apologies for using government force to reshape society in whatever way is fashionable. I'm not falling for it ever again and I want to spread the philosophy of freedom to anyone who'll listen. I left the Left; I hate the concept of a "State" or Government" that uses force to limit liberty, because I love liberty which is truly the essence of life!

Ed Zdrojewski
Editor of *Grain Journal*; Champaign, IL

Ed Zdrojewski, 56, is a native of Cleveland, OH and holds a B.A. degree in journalism from Michigan State University. After a long and checkered career working for newspapers, magazines, and public relations agencies, he currently is editor of *Grain Journal*, a trade publication covering grain elevators and feed mills from its office in Decatur, IL. Ed lives with his wife, Penny Watkins-Zdrojewski, and dogs, Buddy and Murphy, in Champaign, IL.

How the Jesuits Killed My Liberalism Without Ever Trying
by
Ed Zdrojewski

My transition from left/liberal to libertarian came at the hands of a certain Father Leonhardt, SJ, a Jesuit theologian teaching in the late 1960s and early 1970s at St. Ignatius High School in Cleveland, OH. That certainly wasn't his intention, and he probably would be appalled to hear what happened.

In my advanced dotage, I am unable to remember Rev. Leonhardt's first name, and it doesn't appear to be available on the St. Ignatius web site. At my 30th class reunion, I was informed by fellow classmates that he had left the Catholic priesthood some years after my graduation in 1973 and joined a mystical lay Christian community somewhere that was not Cleveland. This surprised me, since he seemed pretty committed to being a Jesuit priest at the time. No telling about people sometimes.

I do remember his nickname, however. Among the students at St. Ignatius, he was known as "Lizard" Leonhardt. Mostly that came from his rather large, hooked nose when viewed in profile, and I suppose it was rather cruel, but what can I say? We were a bunch of budding intellectual teenage boys, and teenage boys are like that. Nobody ever called him Lizard to his face, but I suspect he knew he carried that nickname around the six-story neoGothic building on West 30th Street, and he didn't seem to mind. After all, St. Paul called himself lower than the worms, and the good saint was pretty insufferable most of the time, too.

Lizard Leonhardt preached a theology of good works coupled with extreme selflessness. Perhaps extreme self-abnegation might be a better description. Those of us who came of age reading the works of Ayn Rand might call it Altruism Squared.

Unlike the Protestant churches that have always dominated the United States, which preach a doctrine that generally boils down to Salvation by Faith Alone, the Catholics have always maintained that good works must be part of the Salvation formula. You know, charitable stuff like hospitals, orphanages, welfare agencies, and assuring your spouse that that dress really, really doesn't make her look fat.

Lizard's twist on this idea is that while good works are necessary for salvation, they only count for salvation if they are performed from a state of complete selflessness. If you approached your good works with any anticipation of personal gain, it was absolutely worthless and an abomination in the eyes of the Christian God. In fact, if your good works were done in such a way as to completely screw up your life and cause you maximum personal pain, so much the better.

Lizard went so far as to say that if you so much as allowed yourself to feel good about having done something good, even a split second of feeling personal satisfaction, then your good works were worthless, and God hates you for it.

Now, I was pretty young and naïve at the time, so I didn't realize that Lizard's theology of selflessness isn't really Christian. In fact, I've read the Catholic-approved version of the Bible cover to cover several times, and it isn't in there.

No, where Lizard got those notions from is the philosophical works of Immanuel Kant, an 18th century writer I've come to despise over the years.

Now, I was only 16, but something about this viewpoint struck me as seriously WRONG, so one day after theology class, Lizard and I sat down and got into a rather heated discussion about it.

At the time, I had been doing some volunteer work for a group of local activists as part of a school program. They had an office in a walkup flat a couple of blocks from St. Ignatius, and basically, they were trying to find ways to raise money for a free health clinic for local residents. Not that they actually had a health clinic, mind you. That took a whole lot of money, and they were just trying to get it.

Back in those days, in the early 1970s, the Near West Side neighborhood around the Jesuit high school was kind of iffy as far as poverty and safety went. It was definitely lower working class and largely Latino. One day I was sitting in Latin class, taught by an ancient Jesuit in the most boring monotone this side of Senator Everett Dirksen, and old enough to have learned it first-hand from Cato the Elder, when a brick came crashing through the window. "Nice neighborhood," he said, dropping the brick out of the window, and went back to lecturing on the ablative subjunctive or some such.

Since then, the Near West Side business association began insisting on calling the neighborhood "Ohio City," after what it was called when it was settled by refugees from Connecticut in the early 1800s. That seems to have turned the trick. The neighborhood rapidly gentrified, driving up rents to the point where the local residents had to relocate to outer suburbs so far from their jobs that their 10-year-old beater cars couldn't transport them to what jobs they had in the city. I don't know what happened to them after that. Maybe they starved like in Biafra. Today, though, the area is best known for Lola, the flagship restaurant run by Iron Chef Michael Symon, where even I can't afford to eat.

One of my main jobs working for this activist outfit was (illegally) leafleting mailboxes all over the Near West Side with literature about the promised wonders of this free health clinic, and maybe the local residents could spare a quarter or two to get their free health care? I did this on foot, which is how I managed to only weigh 120 pounds back then. Given that this was about "free health care," maybe I'll only weigh 120 pounds again after Obamacare cures my obesity at gunpoint.

One day I was leafleting this street of run-down duplexes off Lake Avenue. I'd just stepped off the porch of one of them and was walking back to the sidewalk when I was grabbed by the shoulder by this poor white trash dude and violently spun around. He held a butcher knife that was at least 12 inches long at my throat and had a wild look in his eyes as he screamed "WHAT DA FUKK DO YOU WANT HERE? TELL ME OR I'LL FUKKIN SLIT YER THROAT!!!"

I had not yet become a Neopagan at that point, but Hermes already was watching out for me with his gift for fast talking.

219

Somehow, I convinced him that I wasn't working for the Cuyahoga County Department of Child Protective Services, and he let go of me long enough for me to hightail it out of there and back to the office.

The odd thing was, though, no one believed me, when I explained what happened and why I had returned with a bagful of brochures. The office director took me into her office, closed the door, and explained that none of these noble oppressed minority people would ever behave like that, and if I ever told this story again, why, who knows what would happen? I wasn't sure quite what she meant by that and was too young to have heard about re-education camps. Not that there are any, actually, but people like her sincerely hope that someday there will be for people like me.

But that was pretty typical for most of my co-volunteers, right down to high school age. There were a couple of people who actually laughed and joked about stuff in that office—interestingly, both were Latino—but most of the people there never laughed, ever. They seemed to regard laughter as a betrayal of collectivist principles. They were quick to jump down your throat over any remark, however innocent, that they regarded as somehow politically incorrect. They were constantly complaining about the city or county or state for not seeing the value of their work and showering them with taxpayer's money. They were even more constantly complaining about their potential clients for being ungrateful ignoramuses who could not see the benefit of the activists' wise counsel derived from bachelor's degrees in social work. They almost never had anything positive to say about, well, anything. All the time, they professed the kind of extreme selflessness that would do Lizard Leonhardt proud, if he would ever allow himself to feel something so hateful to God as pride.

In other words, the activists in this office came across as some of the most desperately frustrated and unhappy people I had ever met.

I explained this at some length to Lizard and told him I was having trouble with a spiritual philosophy that seemed to make people so unhappy.

When I was done, he looked me straight in the eye and said, "Ed, you're not supposed to be happy. Happiness is for the next life."

At that instant, I knew in my heart that I had ceased to be a Christian.

What I didn't realize at the time and would only come to learn later with much more study and learning is that at that instant, I had also ceased to be a left-wing liberal.

The Christian part was pretty simple. Why would anyone in their right mind worship some H.P. Lovecraft-style monster Yog-Sothoth deity who wants to make people unhappy? I mean, we don't worship cancer, do we? We don't worship street gangs. We don't worship blowouts on the interstate at 70+ mph. All of these things are notable for making people unhappy. If that's what Yahweh Jehovah wants, well, fukkim, and fukk His damnable religion, too!

The left/liberal thing was a bit more complicated. I hadn't at the age of 16 quite made the connection between Lizard Leonhardt's Kantian version of Christianity and the left liberalism of activists who mostly ranked Christianity somewhere between the morality of cops in Grant Park in 1968 and picking your nose and eating it.

You see, back in those days, the late 1960s and early 1970s, a left-winger was the cool thing to be. I called myself a socialist. I even prided myself on having forced myself to wade through the entire length of *Das Kapital*, though I had never thought about the implications.

What about the Soviets, you might ask. What about a so-called left-wing government that diagnosed political opponents as psychotic, locked them in insane asylums, and treated their psychosis with hot sulfur enemas?

What about them, was my glib reply. The Soviets weren't *real* socialists. Marx explained that after we had established the workers' state, the state would, over time, fade away, and we wouldn't need government any more. (Already the budding libertarian anarchist that I am today.)

To be honest, I wasn't cuing off the *Communist Manifesto*. I was cuing off of the 1960s counterculture, which eventually became something quite different from what it originally was. What it originally was was radical individualists—a bunch of ragtag poets and artists and whatnot doing whatever they pleased without first asking the authorities if it was OK. Even Barry Goldwater recognized the value of this, bless his late proto-libertarian heart.

As far as I was concerned, the hippies had a lot going for them. To begin with, they were extremely opposed to the Vietnam War. So was I. (So were most budding libertarians at the time.) Granted, it was kind of personal. My dad was very fond of regaling me with stories about that 12-week Marine boot camp, which sounded like my worst ever gym class multiplied by about 100 in terms of pain and humiliation. (Funny how he would never talk about his experiences in Korea during the Korean War.) I also wasn't fond of the idea of my blood becoming a snack for leeches in a swamp outside of Khe Sanh.

Personal or not, though, I had allies.

Leaving the war aside, the counterculture of the time was remarkably hedonistic, which suited me just fine. They liked to smoke marijuana, and so therefore, there was no reason that marijuana shouldn't be legalized. And they were into sex. Lots of sex. So they didn't have a lot of sympathy for the cops who dragged kids from their cars at that favorite parking spot overlooking Lake Erie and beat them.

None of these viewpoints would be a problem for most libertarians.

Was it a kind of shallow version of libertarianism? Sure it was. Let's face it—wanting to get to second base with your date in the parking lot of a Baptist Church in Cleveland Heights just doesn't have the same sophistication as contemplating the integral equations Ludwig von Mises uses to prove why free markets work better than centrally planned economies. But hey, you have to start somewhere, and teenage hormones are as good a place as any.

Finally, the New Left had the coolest rhetoric. It was in your face and rebellious and outrageous and a great deal of fun to any kid who hadn't taken the time to really think about its implications. You got to say things like "Death to the Fascist Insect!" to adults in authority. How cool is that? I mean, what slogans did the conservatives have? "God made Adam and Eve, not Adam and Steve." C'mon, gimme a break!

There were problems, though, and the more I hung out with the lefties, the more I saw.

One was that the liberals seemed to have a lot of problems dealing with the truth, whenever it was inconvenient for them. Not that they had any monopoly on that—this was during the Nixon administration, after all, and I don't have to tell you about him. But you *would* like your side to be a little better than that.

I discussed the aforementioned health activist who didn't want to believe that the noble poor might actually assault me on the street. The lefties also didn't want to believe that the small business owners and shopkeepers on the Near West Side were actually providing the only paying jobs many of the local residents could get, even though this was painfully obvious to anyone observing the neighborhood without lying to themselves. Those business owners actually made *profits*, and you didn't get any of those without heartlessly exploiting someone, I was told. There were city and county jobs, of course, which by their non-profit nature must be more virtuous—but you couldn't get those jobs without some kind of connection with people in power, which most of the residents of the neighborhood didn't have and would never get.

They also couldn't grasp the concept that you might want to pick and choose the issues you wished to work on. For example, I was with them on ending the Vietnam War "by any means necessary" 100 percent. But that was never good enough for the lefties. You had to be with them on *all* the issues. If you were genuinely against the war, you also had to be for confiscating the wealth of rich people and distributing it to the poor. *And* for sending those people to re-education camps. *And* for shouting down anyone you didn't agree with without

223

ever listening to them. *And* for making everyone eat a vegetarian diet. *And* for outlawing cars and walking everywhere, preferably in your bare feet. *And. . . and . . . and . . .*

And if you weren't with the lefties on any one of these and a whole host of other issues, you were a worthless human being, and everyone should shun you, until maybe you graduate from one of those re-education camps.

I never actually saw any re-education camps and suspect they were a left-wing urban myth, but the whole mindset seemed remarkably effective at creating a permanent state of guilt, self-doubt, frustration, and a generally miserable existence. In fact, it was remarkably like what Lizard Leonhardt was pushing!

Over time, I saw the Left gradually abandon all of the hedonistic stuff that made them so attractive in the first place. The original hippies that came out of California in the early to mid-1960s were heavily into radical individualism, but then they started studying Marx and later literary criticism theories, and they came to realize that individuality was the sign of the Oppressor. Marijuana? You couldn't infiltrate the Democratic Party that way and get into positions of power if you were stoned. Free sex? The radical feminists came along and taught the Left that all heterosexual sex was rape. Art for art's sake? All art is political, and if it didn't tow the leftist line, it was a tool of the Oppressor.

Not too long after my fateful encounter with Lizard, I discovered Ayn Rand, and a whole other world opened up for me—yeah, yeah, Catholic to Objectivist, very cliché, but there you are. Ayn Rand had her problems, of course, but she led to David Friedman. That led to David's daddy, Milton. That led to Hayek and von Mises, though it took a while to master the calculus.

By the time I was a sophomore at Michigan State University, I was pretty much a libertarian. There were some costs. "You used to call yourself a socialist!" wailed my soon-to-be-ex-girlfriend. A lot of old friends cut me off, both in East Lansing and in Cleveland. I found new ones. They were just fine.

A lot of my personal tastes remained rather leftist—scruffy neighborhoods, cluttered apartments and houses (mainly with books), organic foods, indie rock. Years later, I lived in the Rogers Park area on the far north side of Chicago, so naturally, I hung out at a restaurant, bar, and organic product emporium in the area called Heartland Café. It was suitably scruffy and cluttered. It also had a world-class collection of beers in bottles and on tap.

One night I was busy sampling a selection of those beers while seated next to a rather talkative gentleman. He was a life-long left-wing activist and had spent more than a dozen years working for some city-funded social service agency on the South Side. (No, it wasn't Barack Obama.) He'd never had a promotion, although it wasn't clear that there were any promotions available, or that he'd know what to do with a promotion if he ever got one. Nevertheless, he resented that no one in city government appreciated him. Conservatives called him a social parasite. The office where he worked had a leaky roof, and the air conditioning never worked properly, and there was never any money available to fix anything. In fact, his boss had to go in front of the City Council every year and beg like a homeless person for an appropriation to keep the program going. Not that he had any respect for her. The "slut" wouldn't go out on a date with him if she were paid handsomely, and now she had a live-in boyfriend! And the clients? Don't get him started. They were ignorant, and they stank, and sometimes used threatening language if they didn't get what they wanted. They were so ill-educated that they had trouble filling out those five- or six-page application forms without help.

It became more and more clear that this guy had a miserable life, was desperately unhappy, and probably so self-unaware that he could never admit it to himself. The perfect Lizard-Leonhardt-by-way-of-Immanuel-Kant Christian and liberal.

Yet more evidence that back in 1971, I had made exactly the right choice.

About the Compiler and Editor:
Tom Garrison

I am the youngest of four children to two Dust Bowl Okies who migrated to Shafter, California in the Central Valley. My family was fairly apolitical, with Republican leanings. I graduated with a BA in political science from California State College, Bakersfield in 1974 (magna cum laude); earned a MA in political science from University of California, Davis in 1976; and finished everything but my PhD dissertation (ABD) in political science at University of California, Santa Barbara in 1980.

I began political life as a typical McGovern liberal, moved left to become a card carrying member of the Socialist Party USA, and in the late 1990s evolved into a libertarian.

During undergraduate and graduate studies I was active in on-campus politics. As a graduate student at UC Santa Barbara in the late 1970s I led the Graduate Students Association in joining the nationwide Coors beer boycott and several other political campaigns.

In 1972 I joined the War Resisters League and participated in and organized anti-war protests, including giving public speeches before crowds numbering in the hundreds at UC Santa Barbara. For more than 15 years I protested a portion of my income taxes as being war taxes. In the latter years of that period, I withheld part of my income taxes from the federal government.

In 1980 I was arrested, along with hundreds of others, for civil disobedience at the Diablo Canyon nuclear power plant. From the early 1980s to the mid-1990s I was a hyper-active socialist: twice running for Santa Barbara City Council openly as a socialist in the mid-1980s; worked with tenants (three city-wide rent control campaigns in seven years), and gays and lesbians (Deb, my wife, was the first heterosexual on the Gay and Lesbian Resource Center Board of Directors); and fighting political cultists in California's Peace and Freedom Party (the only socialist party with ballot status in California). During this period I also found time to work full-time as an editor (from 1982 to 2000) of a political science journal published in Santa Barbara.

I believe my transition from leftist activist to libertarian, while not common, is instructive. Why would someone abandon a strong belief system, lose many comrades/"friends", and suffer the loss of much of his social network? Why, because I grew to see that the Left (and its handmaiden liberalism) lacked respect and understanding of the concept of personal responsibility; lying was an all too common occurrence that undermined the democratic process; leftists/liberals slavishly adhered to affirmative action preferences, quotas, and identity politics; and leftists/liberals—while embracing "diversity"—all too often display an intolerance for a real diversity of ideas. In 1997 I joined the Libertarian Party.

From the early 1980s to 2000, I published several political articles in publications such as *Liberty* magazine, the *Santa Barbara News-Press*, the *Santa Barbara Independent*, *The Socialist*, *Left Out*, and *Tenants United*.

Beginning in 2000, and for most of the next decade, I mostly dropped out of politics and focused on my job (Real Property Appraiser for the Santa Barbara County Assessor's Office); building a real estate "empire" (four rental condos); and exploring and hiking the southwestern United States with Deb as often as we could get away.

In the last three years (since 2010) I have concentrated on compiling and editing *Why We Left the Left* and publishing essays in regional newspapers—*The Salt Lake Tribune* and the *The Spectrum* (local St. George daily newspaper). The majority of my 35 published articles (as of August 2013) are hiking/travel stories along with some political and humorous essays.

From October 2011 to July 2012 I had a once-a-week 30-minute talk radio show (as a segment of Jake Shannon's two hour "Mental Self-Defense" program) on station KTKK (630 am) covering the Salt Lake City area. I discussed libertarian perspectives on a variety of issues.

Contact me via email at whywelefttheleft@yahoo.com. Also visit the Why We Left the Left Facebook page. Comments are welcome.

8211957R00123

Made in the USA
San Bernardino, CA
31 January 2014